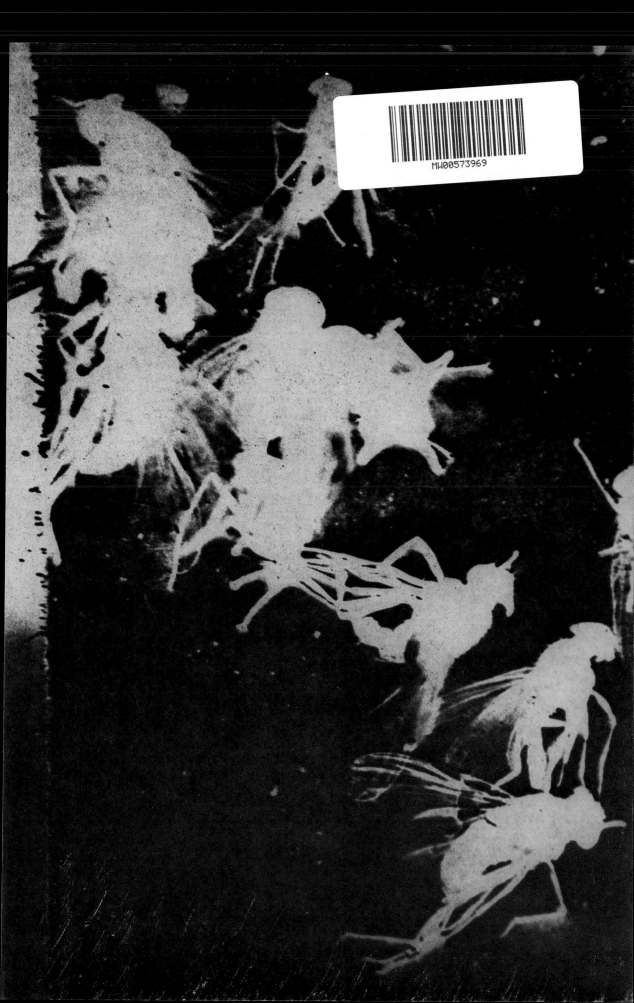

PLATES

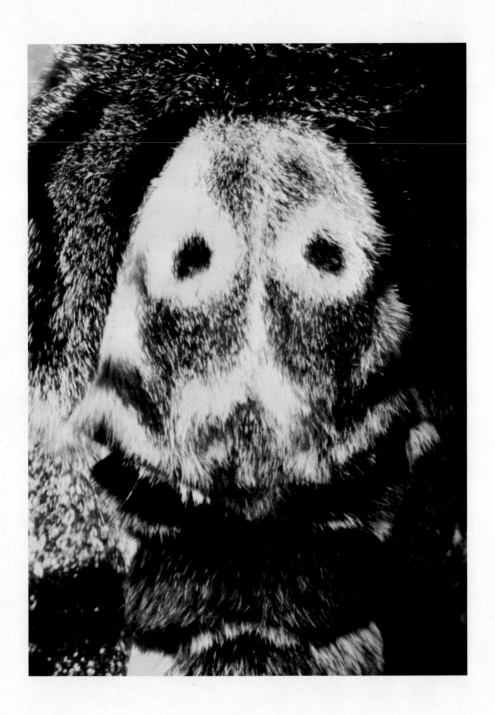

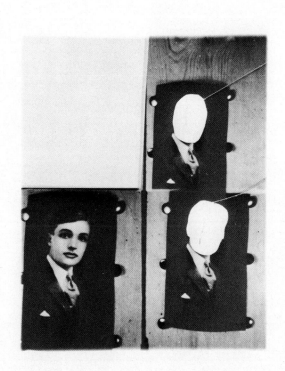

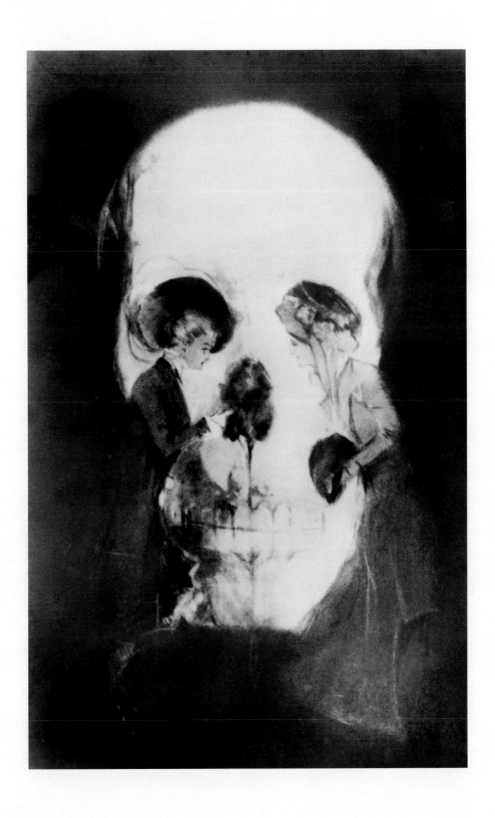

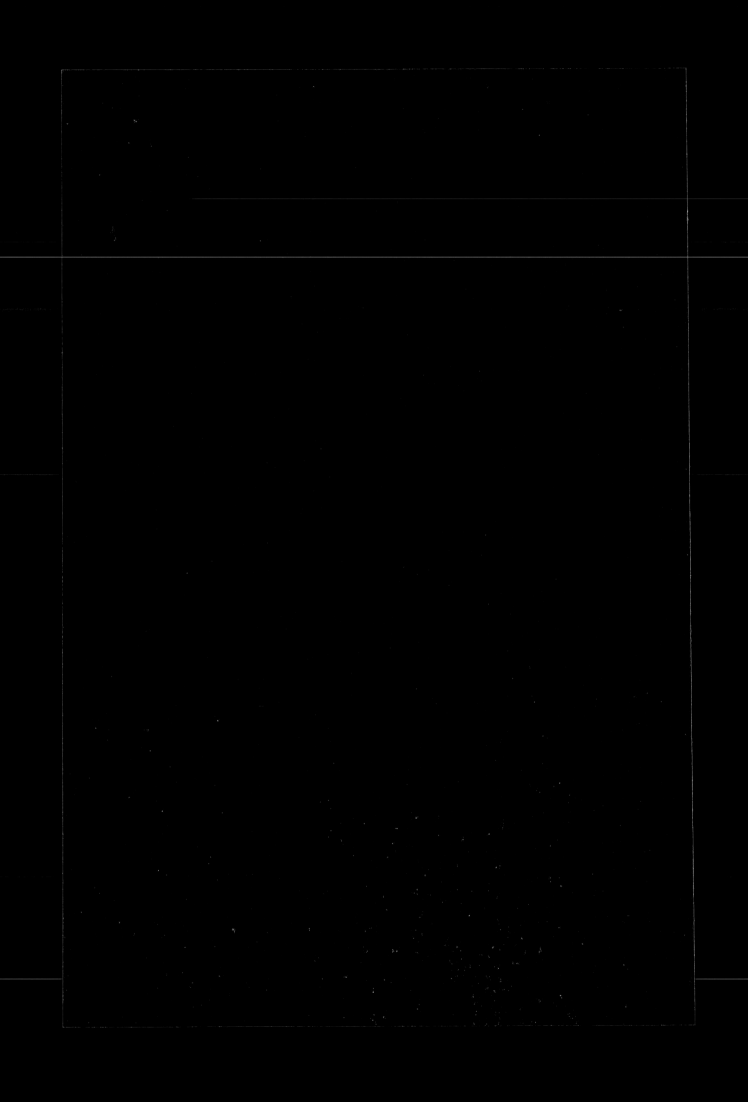

THE NECESSITY
OF THE MIND

AN ANALYTIC STUDY OF
THE MECHANISMS
OF OVERDETERMINATION
IN AUTOMATIC
AND LYRICAL THINKING
AND OF THE DEVELOPMENT
OF AFFECTIVE THEMES IN
THE INDIVIDUAL CONSCIOUSNESS.

PRELIMINARY DEFINITION

The application of scientific rigor and method to a domain where it seems that both its advocates and its deprecators have agreed it has no right to be will very likely displease both parties. This is why it is important to offer a preliminary definition of the movitation for this study and of the goals pursued by its author.

The intentional was to provide an initial, no doubt elementary survey—but one that was at least *direct* and *carefully situated*—of a certain mode of thinking. This work, then, aims to do nothing less—but also nothing more—than to account for the workings of the complex phenomena that we can classify under the heading of *affective imagination* because of their irreducibly double representative and emotional nature, and that seem to make up the substance of the mental attitude generally called *lyricism*, even though no one has been able to provide a coherent ideology of this important concept. It seemed very insufficient and consequently very dangerous to the author to isolate an activity in this way by baptizing it with a word that does not define it, or at least no longer defines it. Perhaps if the mechanisms that form the object of this study had been called *lyrical thinking* and not *lyricism,* a number of crude and incomprehensible errors, the first and foremost of these being the exceptionally unintelligent concept of *pure poetry*, would have been avoided.

For this reason, if a certain well-defined "poetry" is justified, not to say exalted, in the propositions that follow, very specific reservations have nonetheless been expressed with respect to it, even when it is stripped beforehand of all its mystery and aura and reduced to a commonplace. The author, who has used the word as little as possible, thinks that it should be banished for the same sad reasons that force one to adopt a polemical stance with regard to all forms of art and literature such as they have always been, and still are, practiced and conceived. This condemnation is all the more serious given that the person making it admits that with respect to their essence, they have been, and still are, practiced and conceived in an extremely remarkable manner, which is in general a great tribute to human intelligence.

These few lines are a sufficient warning that the author has deliberately adopted a scientific point of view, and that he consequently wishes to hear of no value given to his work other than the rehetorical and documentary interest it might offer. He wanted to give, exactly and objectively, a kind of panormaic and dynamic picture of a psychic life — his own — in its lyrical dimension. To this end he has carefully analyzed, without any hope, moreover, that this analysis could be anything but a humble and schematic beginning, several systems of emotional elements. He was thus able to show their genesis, their elective cohesion, and, above all, their need for proliferation over and against everything in which one has to see, in his opinion, the very essence of the lyrical fact.

Because the interdependence and necessity of the associations draw their power from the most intimate emotions and extend to the most fleeting states of consciousness, the author, in order to pursue his work in a more or less concrete and precise manner, has had to exercise extreme indiscretion with regard to his own life, and, in particular, has had to use a certain number of texts and facts from which he will certainly not derive any benefit — quite the opposite — by their being published. He does not regret this publication, however, for suspecting that he will not be followed in the general hypotheses he has believed it possible to infer from his analyses; he would like to think that those whom they would not satisfy could nevertheless benefit from a work that puts at their disposal a series of unfalsified documents on the workings of the mind. These documents are consequently of a quality that the ravages of psychological literature have made deplorably rare, and they are above all documents of which the interpretation itself is, all things considered, in its turn a document.

R. Caillois
(1933-1935)

2

I

THE LYRICAL IDEOGRAM

*Madness has to be measured by the depth or
shallowness of the penetration, and by the ex-
quisite mixture, of demented ideas.*
J. B. Van Helmont ("Traité des Maladies,"
chapter 10 in *Oeuvres,* translated by Jean le
Conte, Lyon, 1671, p. 295)

Certain abstract reflections, themselves provoked by a series of
emotive phenomena, led me to pose the problem of the value of poetic
expression in a very interested way, and only consequently did they lead
me to study the mechanisms of overdetermination in lyrical and obsessional thinking. It seems to me instructive at this point to present them
succinctly before proceeding to a concrete analysis, so that from the
outset the chronological development appears consistent with the logical deduction, and the transformation consistent with the interpretation.

These pseudo-theoretical considerations were the following: the
relationships of objects to each other, of people to one another, of
objects to people, of ideas to objects, of feelings to ideas and objects,
and so on. All revealed themselves upon examination to be far more
complex than language tends to lead us to believe they are. When one
thinks that the affective development of people's representations is probably the most decisive metamorphosis imaginable they will undergo

and the most irremediably singular with respect to others, one is dumb-founded by the immense relative stability of the instrument they have at their disposal with which to express this development, that is to say, language. Now, it is a cause of immediate terror to think that not only individuals find language ready made, but also to make the least word understood, they are forced to sacrifice all the particular, concrete nuances of their personal experiences to the fiduciary meaning that, for better or for worse, has been generally granted to this word. Under these conditions this word merely represents the ideal and abstract common denominator of a growing multiplicity of perceptions and sensations that are often barely differentiated, but that are always infi-nitely distanced from any absolute identity. When one thus opposes the concrete, singular, and mobile nature of the realities of a consciousness to the abstraction, generality, and permanence of the meaning of words, one understands why the latter has been consigned to dictionaries and why the former has thought up another means of expression that would better respect its inexhaustible complexity and its specific nature: a lyrical language, which is experienced directly through dreams and reflexively through madness.[1] For this use of lyrical mechanisms by the waking consciousness to be valid, it must be surrounded by certain provisions designed to eliminate the action exerted on it by disciplines derived from language, principally those of logic and psychology, an intervention that would provoke more confusion and sacrifice than ever and from which one would therefore have everything to fear. Now, it is a fact that not only does one generally not take any precautions, but also that this displaced use, which is by no means free from the afore-

---

[1] On this bringing together of dream and life, see the forgotten study by J. Moreau (of Tours): *De l'identité de l'état de rêve et de l'état de folie* (Annale Médic.-psych. 1855) [*On the Identity of the States of Dreaming and of Madness*].

4

mentioned contaminations, also continues to benefit, in the name of poetry, from a dubious indulgence that tends to bestow dangerous advantages on it by safeguarding it from even the least precise or rigorous examination, on the pretext that this is a sacrilegious intrusion. Lyrical thinking has more to lose than to gain from such leniency, for one has only to assume that it lives off this indulgence for it to be immediately disqualified. So many works, in fact, present themselves as "poems" when it is difficult to find anything in them but the most inexcusable sentimental, artistic, or intellectual swindle, that it is impossible for a rigorous mind not to consider "poetry" to be the right granted to anyone to say anything without any guarantee, or any obligation, to be held accountable. This is why the slightest compromise demotes poetry to the rank of a literary genre that is particularly literary, and that is scarcely worthy of attention beyond a generally irritating typographical arrangement, except by virtue of its great confusion and an even greater boldness in its pomposity and fraudulence. This state of affairs could therefore be invoked by those with a vested interest, in order to justify the opposition they delight in creating between the poetic, as a special case of the imaginary, and the real. It is nevertheless certain that this situation alone is likely to render surrealism's claims to an absolute objectivity somewhat equivocal, and to force it to enter into unfair and unfounded competition with scientific activity (leaving aside for the moment the prejudicial question of the true consequences of this concept of unfair competition). On the contrary, it is precisely to the extent that surrealism has considered lyrical thinking as a fact, and has systematically exhausted it as such by taking it to its extreme limits — limits that are in their turn lyrical facts capable of being developed concentrically and so forth — that it has properly earned the right to undertake with some validity the critique of empirical imagination.

It is therefore a question of *organizing poetry*. Under these conditions the concept and the object are really equally valid and applicable points of reference, given that between the concept and all the singular adventures that are its affective support there is the same *concrete independence,* the same disquieting relationship as there is between the object and its utilitarian rôle, so that one is a long way from being able to perceive in either case the perfect coincidence that rational thinking assumes them to have. It is obvious that the utilitarian rôle of an object never completely justifies its form, or to put it another way, that the object always exceeds its instrumentality. Thus it is possible to discover in each object an irrational residue determined among other things by the unconscious representations of its inventor or technician.[2] Likewise, every concept possesses a specific concrete value that allows it to be considered as an object and no longer as an abstraction. For example, as an abstraction, the word *spider* can only be taken as a convenient and approximate means of expression. This is the ordinary way of conceiving literature; it is characterized by a hasty and thoughtless use of words that takes only their most superficial, sketchy, and least perceptible qualities, only considering a minimum number of their representations, both personal and impersonal, both obscure and distinct. Its scientific importance is thus rendered, without the least partiality, as good as nonexistent. Poetry, on the other hand, begins the moment the word is considered in terms of the theoretically infinite number of its representations; that is, in the above example, the irrational concept of *spider* is considered as an aggregate of empirical data. Clearly, the affective independence of the concept is determined, with respect to the word that supports it, at the same time 1) by the object, that is, by its potential for collective representation or excitation (just as psychoanalysis and Gestalt-theory reveal the existence in different areas of symbols and forms of attraction that have a universal value); 2) by the

---

[2] There would obviously be an enormous theoretical interest in *isolating* this irrational residue. But in practical terms the operation would be extremely delicate. Only a simultaneous use of different methods and a comparison of their results would allow for any certainty to be reached. Despite a certain lack of technical refinement, surrealist questionnaires could be considered a preliminary stage of investigation.

subject, that is, by the conscious and unconscious systematization of its memories and tendencies or, in a word, by its life; and finally 3) by their previous relationships, that is, by the *"décor"* of the occasions in which they have already been found to be present: spiders' webs destroyed as one advances in the dark; those that Heliogabalus ordered to be collected before nightfall; the legs of the spider known as a daddy-long-legs, which wriggle for a long time in one's open hand; erudite works written on spiders; spiders that prisoners tame in their cells; spiders and sleepwalking; spiders and dishes that have to be eaten cold.[3]

Lastly and above all, the absolute opposition of the lyrical to the real has become difficult to defend. One could at most admit that an industrialized civilization discredits, to the advantage of its own very particular interests, the least immediately useful manifestations of reality to its way of thinking (dreams and madness, for example), and that it puts them into categories such as "the unusual" or "the abnormal," at least as long as these categories involve a purely statistical or commercial judgment. But when an abusive deviation has succeeded in generally imposing the concepts of "appearance" and "subjectivity" — that is, in picking out a certain number of manifestations of reality and declaring them less real than others for the sole reason that they are apparently less dependent on the other representations, that they are of interest only to an individual consciousness or, to top it off, that they are the result of chance—depending on the case, it is a hypocritical confession or a convenient outright refusal, and it then becomes imperative to denounce such arbitrariness and to affirm once and for all that

---

[3] The previous lines are taken largely from an article published in May 1933 in issue number 5 of *Le Surréalisme au service de la révolution (Surrealism in the Service of the Revolution)*, in which I set out schematically the aims of the present work and the situation of surrealism in general from this perspective, and the conclusions of which I present (most of the time I have replaced the words *poetry* and *poetic* by less equivocal terms).

within a philosophy that makes no special provision for the mind, the concepts of appearance and subjectivity can have no meaning.

This being said, the efforts of surrealism will perhaps be easier to situate: people may have believed that it attempted to discredit reality, or more precisely, to put all objective solidity into doubt, with supporting evidence to back this up. This proposition is only correct from a dialectical point of view, if the antithetical aspect of this effort is taken into consideration at the same time: the recognition of the credibility of everything that industrial and rational pragmatism had tried to exclude from reality without ever noticing the pretentious absurdity of such a suppression. Surrealism can thus take as the maxim of its experience Hegel's self-evident aphorism: "Nothing is more real than appearance considered as appearance." This aphorism is also the epigraph of all poetry, which refuses to take advantage of its artistic privileges in order to present itself as a science. Poetry then becomes violently unilateral on principle, siding with the marvelous and the unusual; and it strives, independently of any other consideration and by whatever means, to take into account the irrational element within the object and the concept. But there is nothing for which it will not be accountable, after the fact, to the strictest of methodological critiques.

Along this journey, the presence of mind, which is so useful in other instances, gives way to a mysterious *absence of mind,* and the alleged and illusory independence of mind, which is so brilliant in other cases, gives way to the *necessity of mind*—which is less forgiving and knows better. Lyrical thinking does not have the right to autonomy.

Two equally important results become apparent at the end of this analysis: first, a revision of the abstract-concrete division, which, on a purely empirical level, allows the understanding of a word to be assimilated with that of a concept and that of a concept with that of an object, such that any conscious apperception can be designed by a common term, that of *ideogram.* According to the dictionary definition, this term refers to "signs presenting images of idea or of things." It appears to be perfectly appropriate for this usage, especially if one is careful to qualify it with a modifier such as *mental* or *emotive,* so that one does not mistakenly confuse it with the hieroglyphic writing of ancient Egypt. Secondly, however hasty the above analysis was, it has brought to light an appreciable consistency in the empirical origin of the perceptions that have just been called ideograms, such that from one or more latent systems of association, several series of intellectual, affective, or motor representations are produced that in theory all link up indefinitely to one another and lead to all the others without exception. Moreover, there is no doubt that from a certain relatively minimal distance, these entangled links cease being perceived by a lucid consciousness, even if no directed activity intervenes to inhibit their determinism proper.

Furthermore, each person's experiences tend to set up a hierarchy among these representations for the individual's use. Indeed, during a lifetime, the same object may have presented itself in various relationships to a given individual in circumstances that were moving in varying ways, the object being the only element common to them. By virtue of this fact, this object or concept assumes in emblematic value in relation to the subject; that is, it no longer acts upon the latter solely through the immediate representations it triggers but is also able to arouse, no less immediately and without any further intermediary, a certain number of emotive images, which build up a considerable affective charge with the subject. The ideogram thus possesses a specific double capacity to expand and to integrate, which is the only reason it earns the epithet of "lyrical" if one agrees that it is the imperative of exaltation, and not some musical or aesthetic quality, that must define lyrical thinking. From then on the ideogram enriches itself and becomes more and more pregnant. It can even become tyrannical and can to a certain extent act upon the subject independently of the subject's will, its appearance in a dream being the first manifestation of this independence. Indeed, by virtue of its great emotive potential, the ideogram becomes capable (as in the case of erotic fetishism) of arousing astonishing passional reactions and of monopolizing, so to speak, the consciousness. Under these conditions, it is not surprising that the ideogram does not remain a simple and obedient psychic representation; by intervening in a dream it has already imposed itself in the manner of a hallucination, that is, as a *perception* and no longer as a *representation*. It is true that on waking this perception without an object has once again become a representation, but this is the case for any memory of a perception. The important thing is that the ideogram, for a certain period of time and during sleep, one of the principal modalities of psychic life, was *perceived*. It would no more occur to people to think of discussing its objective reality than it would to discuss that of common objects when one is awake. People have often remarked that while one is dreaming, one's dream is the supreme reality. So it is that the ideogram, as a mental representation, very often acts (with the assistance of the dream, it is true) as if it were part of the outside world, and it manifests a complete autonomy with respect to the subject's will. It is sometimes possible for the subject to extend the same prerogative to a waking state: a hallucination is then produced, that is, a perception that is ultimately differentiated from other perceptions only by virtue of the fact that it is perceived by a single subject and not by everyone, but for the subject it is completely indistinguishable from other perceptions. People suffering from hallucinations unanimously agree that all efforts to reduce hallucination to a consecutive, interpreted image or to a mental image have failed.[4] The point to remember here is that the ideogram reveals itself to be capable not only of taking on an obsessional character and of provoking astonishing

---

[4] As concerns this debate it is worthwhile, and even perhaps salutary, to find out more precisely about the state of current professional psychology, both empirically and theoretically. Simple souls could be in for quite a surprise. I refer the reader on this subject to volume 2 (Clinical Studies) of the recent and remarkable work by Pierre Quercy, *L'Hallucination* (Alcan, 1930).

deliriums of interpretation—thereby appropriating, already in a quite remarkable manner, qualities belonging to the sensible—but also of occupying the entire space of a perception to the point where a subject, far from being able to assimilate the ideogram as a psychic representation, experiences it as the independent and objective exteriority of an object. This hallucinatory objectivization, which takes extremely diverse forms, some of them very frequent and even experienced daily, is extremely serious when one thinks that if it was not for the fact of the person suffering from the hallucination being the only one to perceive it, no one would have the empirical means of distinguishing it from a perception, so that one would have to wonder whether every object does not have an endogenous origin: this would make the already very complex relationship of consciousness to the external world truly inextricable. This being the case, one ought to reflect upon the thought that, because everything leads us to believe there is only a difference of degree and not of nature between what we agree to (vaguely) name matter and spirit, objectivity and subjectivity (an irreducible dualism being scarcely imaginable), it is not impossible for a consciousness to be endowed with enough power and contamination to cause other consciousnesses that are just as impassioned to contract almost instantaneously, with respect to the ideogram that interests such a consciousness, the same effective, objectivizing hallucinatory capacity as that by which it is possessed.[5] So that if the final recourse indicated above—the fact that the hallucination would only be perceptible to the person suffering from the hallucination—was abolished, the situation

---

[5] The image commonly acts through a sort of *lyrical authority,* which seems to be very easily assimilable to the phenomenon of hypnotic suggestion. Now, in hysteria even nonhypnotic suggestion can, as Charcot concludes (corroborated on this point, and doubtless on this one alone, by Balinski), "take considerable proportions and ultimately end up objectively producing the imagined symptoms" (see Dr. J. Vinchon, *Hystérie,* Stock, 1925, p. 105 [*Hysteria*]). Likewise in psychoanalysis, purely psychic treatments can cure spasms, tumors, paralysis, and lesions.

previously described would be realized: the mental and supposedly inner world of representation would be *objectively* confused with the physical and supposedly outer world of perception—at least on the particular point of the envisaged ideogram—all due to a process of true lyrical materialization.[6]

---

[6] I am not proposing any factual observations here, even though they would not be difficult to find. I am merely interested in studying the development of a phenomenon *when the conditions of which it is a function vary indefinitely in the same direction,* which corresponds exactly to the problem in mathematics of the passage to the limit. In both the former and latter instances, such an examination has no practical consequences; one cannot even conclude from it whether the envisaged passage to the limit is practically attainable. A schematic knowledge of it is no less necessary for a complete understanding of the curve or of the phenomenon in question in the relatively narrow field in which we are at liberty to study it more surely, using ordinary calculation or the data of everyday experience.

II

THE OVERDETERMINATION OF IDEAS

After defining the dynamic element of mental life, and after showing briefly how one could call upon it to tackle the most immediately
appealing questions, we should now examine more attentively the
mechanisms of its formation and development. Such a study clearly
coincides in part with the traditional problem of the association of
ideas. The sorry state in which this problem has remained is also well
known. It was assumed that one representation evoked another in accordance with certain laws, but the laws that were discovered were so
vague that they allowed any representation whatever to induce more or
less any other, such that one was no more advanced than before, to the
great joy of advocates of psychological freedom.

While reflecting on this failure, it occurred to me that the psychoanalytic concept of overdetermination could be extremely useful in
resolving the problem, and that in any case it matched up well with my
conception of the lyrical ideogram, which from this point of view was
nothing but a particularly overdetermined representation.[1] This assimilation of the lyrical ideogram in a waking state to the overdetermined

---

[1] See Freud, *The Interpretation of
Dreams,* "The Dream of the Botanical
Monograph," trans. James Strachey (New
York: Avon Books, 1965), pp. 316-318.

image in the dreaming state led me to try to discover how the mechanism of the association of ideas was overdetermined, because the latter seemed to me to correspond exactly, from one state to the next, to the identification through condensation, which is a consequence of the former.

A particularly simple dream I had in the meantime afforded me proof (which, to tell the truth, I hardly needed) of this minor and very plausible hypothesis, a proof that is interesting insofar as it helps to show the unity of mental life, but that is really not essential for the present argumentation:

> At night at the place du Châtelet, while waiting for a
> break in the stream of cars—that are now going by bumper
> to bumper—to allow me to cross, I notice a woman
> dressed in black, who is well known. I call her by her first
> name, and she accompanies me or I accompany her down
> along the river. Finally, leaning against the parapet, we
> embrace passionately, and I feel with a singular aesthetic
> precision all of the sensations of a long kiss (which wake
> me up).

I was very struck during and after this dream by the quality of what I would call the *absorbed multiplicity* presented by the female character in my dream adventure. But her truly composite personality, however indissoluble as it may have been perceived, easily allowed the elements of the condensation to be recognized. In the first place, the outer appearance of the creature was that of a woman clearly loved by me, but with whom I had already broken up a long time ago, having finally noticed that she was too concerned with her own very debatable interests for anyone to expect from her the least lyrical behavior. The first name—*Mona*—by which I had called out to her in the dream was the very one I had given her to prevent her being named in the same way by her husband and by myself. However, the way the creature of the dream behaved, her attitudes, her words, her consent, belong with-

14

out any doubt to A., my girlfriend, who presents a contrast to Mona first of all by being of an absolutely different physical type and then, above all, by the fact that in her life she has achieved, as absolutely and as completely as possible, an admirable and, in the present case, often tragic combination of lyrical and moral values. The place where the dream was felt to have occurred also determined her intervention in it: it is the place where once, as night was falling, I, who never kiss a woman in the street, actually kissed her. Finally, I had to connect up the singular way in which the woman of the dream placed and moved her tongue during the kiss to a third person, whose acquaintance I recently made abroad (and whom it is unnecessary to characterize any further, for I will have no more occasion as this study develops to talk of her).

Ordinarily I would no doubt not have given any importance to such a common kind of dream condensation, classified for a long time now and of which I myself had already experienced several fine examples.[2] But absorbed as I was in the preoccupations I mentioned above, I could not fail to notice that the different women, fused into one by the specific condensation process of the dream thought, were people who have had the same relationship to me—the particularly powerful relationship created by erotic affairs—and that consequently my waking thoughts could have connected one to the other without any mediation through an unusually constraining and self-determining association of ideas. The dream thus tended to confirm my hypothesis. At the same time it prompted me—in order to explain the lesser known of the two mechanisms—to use the phenomenon of overdetermination, which explained the other mechanism so satisfactorily and at the same time I

---

[2] See Freud, *The Interpretation of Dreams*, "Collective Figures," p. 327.

could use so precisely to account for the formation of the lyrical focal points I had just named "ideograms."

It was while thinking about this that I also became acquainted, at least fairly well, with the paranoiaco-critical study that Salvador Dali was just finishing on the *Angelus* of Millet. Of course there it was a matter of essentially delirious interpretations, which were a long way from offering the meticulous rigor of automatic determination that I was attempting to discover beneath the apparent arbitrariness of the antiquated association of ideas. However, despite the great lack of necessity and the equally great quantitative inadequacy of overdetermining factors in the linking together of elements (the subjectivity of Dali obviously compensated for this double lack by the paranoid nature of the hyper-evidence that, as he constantly points out, he felt, and he used the experience of this hyper-evidence to energetically counter my objections), this work presented on the whole so many interferences and intersections that it appeared to me almost immediately that it could be a precious illustration of my conceptions, which at the very least it certainly helped to reinforce.

I then remembered a book I had read and forgotten a long time ago, *Inferno,* in which August Strindberg recounts the innumerable coincidences that marked the short space of time he lived in Paris, and that seem for the most part (although the author denies this) due to the delirious interpretive activity produced by the persecution mania from which he was suffering.[3] This book, published in 1898, aside from its equally striking splendors and shortcomings, is to be recommended for its interest as a log book in which ghostly encounters are recorded without comment. It had made a particular impression on me because

---

[3] See infra., "Supporting and Supplementary Documents," 1, pp. 117-120. This is also the opinion of the psychiatrists Sérieux and Capgras in their work *Les Folies Raisonnantes,* Alcan, 1909 [*Rationalizing Manias*].

[4] On second thought, I believe the idea came to Strindberg while reading the hallucination recounted in a story by Edgar Allan Poe in his *Tales of the Grotesque and Arabesque,* which is precisely about a death's-head moth that climbs up a window and is mistakenly perceived to be of

of a digression on the butterfly named *Acherontia atropos* or more commonly death's-head moth, in which, as both an insect collector and a seeker of the funereal and the supernatural, I had a considerable interest. Profiting from the chemistry and botany research to which he devoted himself in those days in his laboratory near the Rue Campagne-Première, the results of which he recorded respectively in his books *Introduction to a Unitary Chemistry* and *Sylva Sylvarum,* Strindberg scientifically explained in the pages of *Inferno* (based on the places frequented by the butterfly, the plants on which it fed, the chemical analysis of its sap, the trouble with its vision that the sap is liable to produce, etc.) that a mark in the shape of a death's head could be found on the butterfly's corselet; at the same time he discovered a considerable number of natural intersecting lines. At the time I had been especially impressed by the idea of this demonstration, not understanding very well that anyone would think of attempting it, even Strindberg, obviously the man who was the most predisposed to this kind of audacity, he who approached the study of the natural sciences with the mind of a medieval alchemist.[4] When I remembered his demonstration in the circumstances I mentioned above, I was, on the contrary, struck less by the fact that it was conceived than by the fact that it had succeeded to such a great degree. I deduced from this, a little prematurely perhaps, that objective ideograms existed and that overdetermination was at work just as much in the real world as it was in the psychic world, given that Strindberg's pages relied almost entirely on scientifically controlled facts. I therefore concluded that nature in general, and not only the processes of thinking, concealed many intricate subterranean networks of overdetermination.

enormous dimensions. It is also remarkable that in Strindberg's text the presence of the death's head on the butterfly is explained not only by the *same* hallucinatory mechanism, but also by the *same* hallucination. Daniel Rops incidentally points out in *Carte d'Europe* [*Map of Europe*], Perrin, 1928, p. 20) that Strindberg read Poe on the advice of Olas Hanson immediately before coming to Paris.

One can see from this brief overview what an ambitious theory of the entire universe my original concept of the lyrical ideogram led to, which may itself have had its source in my growing aversion to the so-called *pure* forms of art and artistic activity in general and even more in my hostility toward contemporary psychology, whose concepts and disparate frames of reference, characterized by their extreme mutual independence, seemed to me unable to account for the interdependence of all states of consciousness. I had an almost continual experience of this interdependence, which I constantly confirmed to be inconceivably multiple and ramified, and which, on top of all that, I had just extended to the objective world, making up for the inadequacy of my proof by my enthusiasm.[5]

It was in this state of intellectual rapture and confidence in my theory that I answered André Breton's and Paul Eluard's questionnaire for the review *Minotaure: "Can you say what the major encounter of your life has been? To what extent did it, and does it still, give you the impression of something fortuitous and necessary?"* Because this questionnaire posed the question of chance, it corresponded to my most burning concerns. I have transcribed here my answer in its entirety; as it happens, the second part of it is particularly important, at least insofar as it expresses in a strict, coherent, and also overgratuitous manner the results of what I was anticipating:

> *I have never had an encounter which has seemed* DUE
> *to me, in the most inflexible and aggressive sense of the*
> *word, that is to say that nothing which I have been able to*

---

[5] I will subsequently show more clearly and succinctly the reservations I have about, and the sense in which I maintain, the distinction between the objective and the subjective. I will mention here that, in my opinion, it is a question of two poles between which any resolution or continuity is inconceivable.

find out what I call, not without a smile, my way, has ever appeared to me as something encountered. It is impossible for me to see the cause of this in a certain lack of wonder at the happenstances of life, since I am hardly exempt from this undesirable feeling on other occasions. Rather, I must acknowledge that the distant and imperious impartiality, which does not even count me among the superior determinations which it is important to obey a priori, effectively prevents me, less indifferent than they, from experiencing as an encounter that which it can only consider as a common situation possessing a merely illusory privilege over other situations. How can I otherwise explain that those events in my life which had more right than most to be considered as exceptionally gratuituous and decisive encounters, aroused no specific affective resonances within me which would allow them to be distinguished as such from more ordinary meetings?

Similarly the concept of an encounter does not seem to me to be fully worked out on a theoretical level, at least insofar as it assumed the existence of pure, external determinations whose absolute independence would bestow on their interference the qualities of a true encounter, an encounter which would be considered fortuitous or unavoidable, depending on whether one thinks the laws of nature are contingent or necessary. Indeed, we search in vain for the watertight barriers which would allow such perfect isolation. It seems on the contrary that causal series are not only determined, but overdetermined in relation to one another, with the number of overdeterminations, whether recognized or not, increasing all the time. Those coincidences, which it is basically very childish to be surprised at, are thus extremely partial testimonies and infinitesimal revelations of this multiple, subterranean interdependence. Likewise, the few positive investigations

of surrealism are basically just so many methodical at-
tempts designed to uncover the web of lyrical overdeter-
minations, whose rigorous latent systematization does not
allow the so-called encounters to take on the color of the
miracle with which the misunderstanding of their syntax
adorns them. The only true encounters are those which are
mechanical and significant, like the conjunctions of stars. [6]

I fully realized that these lines had hardly any value except as an extrapolation designed to prepare the interpretation of a certain number of phenomena in one sphere, with the help of hypotheses verified in another. This method of exploration appears as a humble and circumspect application of the principles of analogy and continuity, a method used constantly and exclusively by the most rigorous scientific minds, and one that is all the more legitimate in that it is difficult to see how the least theoretical investigation could advance at all without it. It seems to me, in fact, to be a hitherto unjustified expression of optimism to put forward logical deductions and even, to a great extent, dialectical anticipations with a view toward systematization, without any counterbalance in experience. [7] Such dialectical anticipations appear — until they have been more concretely analyzed and more exactly determined — to give just as much freedom, in the guise of suppleness, to the particular prejudices of the dialectician as the directions of common sense give

---

[6] See *Minotaure,* nos. 3-4.

[7] This is a question of general logistics, which has no direct bearing on my study. It seems that as concerns this problem — that of the legitimate use of rational deduction — it would be more reliable, before pursuing this question any further on a personal level, to defer to Kant's quadruple argumentation in *The Transcendental Analytic* on the axoms of intuition, the anticipations of perception, the analogies of experience, and the postulates of empirical thought.

to the prejudices of the person who claims to act in accordance with them.[8]

In short, while keeping intact the validity of my propositions as working hypotheses, I had all the more reason to back them up with analyses that would be as concrete and as well researched as possible. Better still, before attempting to verify them in the world, where they were perhaps the least plausible but also where I unfortunately stood out by my lack of competence, it seemed to me more urgent and more useful to proceed to a complete and detailed elaboration of my concepts in the only world in which I felt at all sure of myself, and at least as well equipped as the next person: the immediate and ideogrammatic world of the affective imagination.

---

[8] These reservations about the way in which one commonly adapts the dialectic (the Hegelian dialectic, of course) to concrete facts are the least that an otherwise well-disposed mind could have. This correlation has until the present time been so manifestly inconsistent and arbitrary that salutary concern about its unqualified value is beginning to be felt in certain interested milieus. See G. Bataille and R. Queneau: "La critique des fondements de la dialectique hégélienne" (*La Critique Sociale,* no. 5, March 1932). None of this, however, affects the necessity of the preoccupation with dialectics, but it is intended to condemn the syllogistic use made of what should only be a state of mind: the thought of each antinomy with respect to an exhaustive synthesis.

III

THE MECHANISMS OF AUTOMATIC THINKING

The modality of the study I was about to undertake was provided for me by the same assimilation that had been my point of departure, namely that waking thoughts, *left to their own necessity* and as a consequence of those particularly rich and compelling representations that were called *lyrical ideograms,* would act exactly like condensed dream images, so that the automatic association of ideas would function according to the same mechanism of overdetermination as the elaborative activity of dreams.

This being the case, I came to the conclusion that the analysis of a spontaneous associative chain, triggered by the intervention of a lyrical ideogram and left to run its own course, could well be the best source of information about the determining elements of this ideogram. It was not lightly that I substituted to this end the use of *automatic thinking* for that of automatic writing, such as it has been defined by André Breton and as I have practiced it. Indeed, it semed to me that automatic writing had not lived up to all that we, in our enthusiasm, had believed it promised.

First of all, to consider it only in terms of its results, it would appear possible to contest the latter by using the crucial set of arguments that the sociological and Marxist schools have used against dogmatic moralism.[1] In any given era, philosophers starting out from op-

---

[1] Particularly Lévy-Bruhl in the preface of his book *La Morale et la science de moeurs,* Alcan, 1903.

posite principles have ended up decreeing the same moral imperatives; at different times, philosophers starting out from identical principles have arrived at different moral imperatives. In the same way, the automatic texts published, for example, in *La Révolution surréaliste,* mutually resemble each other just as the texts obtained by mediums using the same techniques resemble each other. This double resemblance contrasts with the absolute difference separating the former from the latter. How can one avoid thinking, then, that automatic writing, far from reflecting the utmost purity of the mind, not only does not eliminate the constraints of the environment—the dominant pressures of whatever the prevailing fashion and received ideas—but especially insofar as it is *forced,* it encourages their latent influence, at least in terms of form if not of content, if it is true that only a perfect lucidity can check the action of unconscious determinations of which, let us not forget, they are part!

This is why the fact that mediumistic texts show so clearly the effects of spiritualist dogma and that surrealist texts show so clearly the effects of previous aesthetics is a matter for serious concern. Such shortcomings could, however, be merely accidental and might not lead to a condemnation of automatic writing. It seems, on the contrary, that they are the result of a particularly profound difficulty. Indeed, if one examines attentively André Breton's definition of automatic writing,[2] it does not take long to notice that not only does this definition consider resolved a problem that is far from being resolved—the relationship of

---

[2] "*Psychic* automatism in its pure state, by which one proposes to express— *verbally, by means of the written word,* or in any other manner—*the actual functioning of thought. Dictated* by *thought,* in the absence of any control exercised by reason, exempt from any aesthetic or moral concern." *Manifestoes of Surrealism,* trans. Richard Seaver and Helen R. Lane (Ann Arbor: The University of Michigan Press, 1969). p. 26.

[3] See in December 1929, in the *Second Manifesto of Surrealism,* then in the "Letter to Rolland de Renéville" (*Nouvelle Revue française,* 1 May 1932) and very recently in the article entitled "Le Messagge automatique" (*Minotaure,* nos. 3-4, December 1933). This question is really so obvious that those who are the least well placed to pose it have at least to take it into account. Thus Marcel Raymond, whose book *From Baudelaire to*

24

thought to language—but that the solution it implicitly offers is the least defensible one. This is all the more decisive in that this solution happens to be the only one that can provide a basis for automatic writing's capacity to reveal the "actual functioning of thought." Indeed, if one refers to the words I italicized in Breton's definition, one notices that their use constitutes an application of the vocabulary of language to the fact of thought, which amounts to assuming a perfect adequation between these two registers. Yet no one, not even the most intellectual of philosophers, would defend this purely verbal conception of thought, a conception that had always been refuted by the efforts of the most elementary introspective psychology until the discovery of the unconscious rendered it definitively untenable. Thus, it seems to me, one has to come back to this definition, which events have shown to be perfectly adequate for the purposes that its author assigned to it, but which, on preliminary examination and from a strictly ideological perspective, turns out to be incapable of providing a foundation for any work that has the slightest claim to rigor.

The criticism of this crucial text, a revision that had been made indispensable by the very evolution of the surrealist movement toward ever more scientific ambitions and whose necessity it seems André Breton himself felt on several occasions, is much more limited than it seems if one remembers that it is valid only to the extent that (and the measure of this "extent" remains undetermined) thought differs from language.[3] In other words, it basically affects the general spirit of the

---

Surrealism (London: Peter Owen, 1961) can be taken as characteristic of the kind of indulgence that I habitually denounce, is forced to note on p. 291:

> It is extremely doubtful whether the surrealists have succeeded in producing an authentic image of spontaneous dreamlike thought. On the contrary, it seems that in many cases they have set in motion rather superficial mechanisms and

have propagated a current of literary *thought that is almost always "directed," even though this may be contrary to the will of the authors.*

conception very little. This conception seems to me to retain all its value, provided one pays attention less to automatic writing than to *automatic thinking,* by which I mean *the series of spontaneously associated representations or ideas evoked by virture of the lyrical determinism of the ideograms and independently of any external prompting, either from the theoretical demands of conceptual thought or from the utilitarian demands of practical acts, thus independently of any final conscious activity.*

Defined in this way, automatic thinking reminds one more of hypnagogic reveries than of mediumistic speech. But it is, nonetheless, to borrow the terminology of a famous distinction, diffluent and non-plastic, and as a result the problem of its verbal or graphic expression is considerably reduced.[4] In effect, it asks much less of language than does automatic writing, where there always existed a propensity to construct sentences, an entirely artificial concern that unfortunately has nothing to do with the way directed thinking uses syntax. On the contrary, in the case of automatic thinking it becomes a matter of mere transcription, for which a simple linear notation or a pure juxtaposition of the images or memories evoked is all that is needed.

After I had adapted surrealist writing to the exigencies of scientific method, all I had left to do was to let the experiment begin and to analyze the result. An opportunity was, in fact, not long in presenting itself.

---

[4] It is not a matter of indifference to point out that the distinction between the plastic and the diffluent proposed by Ribot in 1900 (*Essay on the Creative Imagination,* trans. Albert H. N. Baron, Chicago: Open Court, 1906), the same year as the publication of Freud's *Interpretation of Dreams,* in order to characterize the two kinds of imagination, should have ended up recently in Tristan Tzara's distinction of poetry as a means of expression and of poetry (*Essai sur la situation de la poésie,* Surrealism A.S.D.L.R. No. 4, pp. 15-23), an activity of the mind that is compared by the author himself to Jung's opposition in *Symbols of Transformation* between directed thinking and nondirected thinking.

At that time I was interested, more than was reasonable, in the game of chess. I was still preoccupied by the fact that in Poland, where I had just spent several weeks, I had wanted to play, but to no avail, until the day before my departure when unexpectedly, during a visit to friends of my host, I was at last able to satisfy my desire *in extremis,* so to speak. I was certainly aware of the emotional ties that attached me to this game and made it a particularly dense ideogram for me, but not having thought about it for a long time, the memory of my recent game alone crossed the threshold of my consciousness. So it was that one evening my mind began to wander, as it often does, from the book I was reading, so that my eyes continued their back-and-forth movement along the lines while my conscious mind drifted off into the most uninhibited and diffuse reverie.[5] The "game of chess" element was suddenly introduced by the anecdote of the impossible reward its inventor asked for, this itself being brought about either by my reflection on geometric progressions or more probably by the fact that I had learned this anecdote in Reims (that is, in the very town I was in once again), where it was told to me by a Persian with whom I in fact used to play chess. What is more, the anecdote supposedly took place in Persia. The ideogram, after it had been activated by this extremely neutral representation, led to the following short series of spontaneous associations, which I noted down immediately and began to analyze straightaway:

---

[5] The book was *Le Vicaire des Ardennes,* a novel H. de Balzac wrote when he was young, of the so-called frenetic genre condemned as detrimental to morality and religion and reduced to pulp by the justice under Louis XVIII. Despite all my efforts, I was able to find nothing in the text my eyes were reading and that I consequently perceived unconsciously that might seem as if it triggered off or influenced the concomitant chain of as- sociations. I am nonetheless giving the reference of the passage to set my mind to rest: chapter 9, approximately from "One day, I had accompanied Mélanie to a place. . . ."

The Bishop Murder Case [Le Fou des échecs], *a detective novel by S. S. van Dine; the atmosphere in advanced mathematics class; Riemann-Christoffel's formula for determining the curvature of hyperspace; the total depreciation of man, a "hydro-carbonated animalcule," as van Dine says in the same book; Pliny the Elder's pessimism and the marvelous; Flaubert's borrowings in* The Temptation of Saint Anthony; *regret that this temptation was a failure; likewise in the novel* Atlantida *by Pierre Benoit, a symmetrical regret and a real anger that Captain Morhange did not give in to Antinea; the brilliant idea G. W. Pabst had in his film; Antinea playing chess; the actress Brigitte Helm; I see Mona again when, knowing that I loved her and seeing that I was going to lose this first game of chess I was playing against her husband, she swept the chessboard with her arm, knocking over all the pieces; this is the gesture of Baron von Kempelen's false automaton chess player, a gesture that I had attributed for a long time to his terrible adversary, the empress Catherine the Great; cruel women sovereigns, Agnes of Hungary, cited by Sacher-Masoch; my conversation on this subject with A, who refused to play chess with me under unusual circumstances." (27 September 1933)*

In theory this series of associations presents no difficulty. Its obsessional character, notably the cyclical return of the "game of chess" element, is maybe a little surprising, but there is really nothing in it that would contradict classical explanations in terms of continuity, resemblance, or affective identity. Such explanations err, therefore, not on the side of excess but of default, remaining particularly incapable of accounting for the choice of the associated element from among all whose association would be equally justifiable. It is precisely this lack that I am concerned to fill.

I. CONJUGATED DETERMINISM

If one examines the chain of associations reproduced above, a chain that was triggered during a particularly relaxed state of consciousness through the intervention of a borrowed element of great emotional power, one notices fairly quickly that not all the representations evoked perform the same function. There is first the lyrical ideogram itself, the chess game, which is a constant, subordinating element; then there are what one might call the principal elements, those that manifestly and immediately contain this ideogram in their concrete multiplicity; and finally, the representations that do not contain the lyrical ideogram make up a third category: that of secondary elements that, in the example in question, bind the principal elements to each other.

It is important to preface this by noting that in directed thinking, that is, when it is a matter of consciously associating emotions or images containing the same element, intentionality is enough to determine what is chosen. A direct link is thus obtained between the elements that contain the representation that has been overdetermined by them, those that are related to it without containing it, having been repressed by the teleological activity of directed thinking. In other words the secondary, intermediate elements disappear, and only the principal elements remain. This being the case, the associative chain is, in a sense, flawless. The associative chain of the chess game would thus be as follows:

> *Van Dine's* The Bishop Murder Case; *Antinea playing chess in the film by Pabst; Mona sweeping clean the chessboard; A refusing to play chess with me.*

The ideogram does connect the representations contiguously, but it in no way determines their order, which remains inexplicable. Indeed, if one indicates the dominant element, with its passional value and emblematic significance, by an *X*, and the representations that contain it by *A, B, C, D,* and so on, one obtains the following schema:

$$\frac{A}{X} \times \frac{B}{X} \times \frac{C}{X} \_\_\_\_ \frac{N}{X}$$

in which the conscious intentionality undoubtedly accounts for the elimination of the secondary elements that have disappeared, but in which it is impossible to notice anything that could justify adopting the order *A, B, C,* and so on to the detriment of the orders *C, A, B,* etc., *C, B, A,* etc., or *B, C, A,* etc.

We must therefore assume that the order adopted is determined by the intermediate elements, which the relaxing of conscious tension in the automatic association allows to appear and whose presence is shown in the "chess game delirium" or the secondary representations *a, b, c, d, e, f, g, h,* and so on. The complete phenomenon can be illustrated by the following new schema:

$$\frac{A}{X} \ a, b, c \quad \frac{B}{X} \ d, e \quad \frac{C}{X} \ f, g, h, i \quad \frac{D}{X} \ etc.$$

a schema that, far from excluding the previous one, implies and completes it. Indeed, the order of the elements in the directed association necessitates a more rigorous system of unconscious associations, but the cyclical nature of these associations in turn presupposes the subordinating and consequently already teleological power of an ideogram. This is why the ideogram occupies exactly the same place in the directed association as the various multiplicities of secondary elements do in the automatic association, to the point where it seems to have done without itself and substituted in its place a series of parasitical representations.

Whatever the case may be, we are in the presence on the one hand of a direct, immediate, and manifest chain of associations—which is, however, already abstract and stereotyped because of the immutable formal identity of the ideogram—and on the other hand of a complex, mediated, and subterranean chain of associations—which is, however, extremely concrete and different each time due to the welter of singular images.

Would not the coexistence of this double determinism, one aspect revealed by directed thinking and the other by automatic thinking, explain the deep-seated mechanism of the association of ideas? Would it not in particular account for its preferential activity, making the choice of the representation evoke the result of rigorous determination and no longer the result of the arbitrariness of the mind?

It seems that this is indeed the case. The confrontation between two schemas, that of the directed association and that of the lyrical association, does not reveal the existence of two superimposed determinisms but, to be more exact—so as not to be tempted to take this expression literally, because it does not of course correspond to any actual dissociation nor, a fortiori, to any superimposition—reveals rather the existence of what one might call a *conjugated* determinism, that is, of a *process inherent in the mechanism of the association of ideas and eminently capable of selection because it acts both from the anterior to the posterior as efficient causality and from the posterior to the anterior as final causality.*

In effect, it seems that the element a, in this case Van Dine's novel *The Bishop Murder Case,* was chosen because it was the only one of all those—a, a', a'', a''', and so on—related to the inductive element A (the chess game), which can lead to the principal element B, that is, "Antinea playing chess," via the secondary evocations, "the scientific depreciation of man," "pessimism and the marvelous in Pliny the Elder," "Flaubert's *Temptation of Saint Anthony,*" and "Atlantida." This principal element is chosen in turn because, of the series *B, C, D, E,* and so on, it is the only one that can be related to A, not only by the presence of the ideogram but also by a concrete series of associations. Similarly the element d, "the actress Brigitte Helm," is induced not because it is related to the inductive element, namely the film by Pabst (there are ten thousand other representations that have as close or as

31

distant a relationship to this film), but because it is related at the same time to the inductive element and to the third principal induced element C, "the gesture of Mona sweeping clean the chessboard." This element also contains the lyrical ideogram, which is defined precisely by its power of integration and performs an inductive function for those very elements that are going to induct it. Thus there is a sort of reciprocal determinism that cannot fail to remind one of the Leibnizian theory of compossibility and of the method used in geometry to determine the location of points that have to satisfy two or more conditions. Neither is it unrelated to evolutionist conceptions of adaptation to the environment and consequently of the survival of the species. Everything, therefore, leads us to believe that this conjugated determinism not only accounts for the association of ideas, but, what is more, also corresponds to deeper processes of the mind and of nature. *In the particular instance of the association of ideas, it is as if there was a determinism that proposes and a determinism that disposes,* the latter being none other than the lyrical power of the ideogram that, in selecting from among all the possible associative detours, the only one capable of inducing in its turn an emblematic and emotional image that contains it and imposes it on one's consciousness, fulfils very precisely the role of the intention or, better still, the *task* of directed thinking.[6] Thus, in automatic thinking the selective mechanism of the association is a truly magnetic psychic force, thanks to which the ideogram annexes, tendentiously and lyrically, the secondary representations linked to it, which are best able to serve its greater glory by resurrecting it from its ashes.[7]

This does not, however, eliminate all obstacles. The previous hy-

---

[6] We are thinking here of the notion of *Aufgabe* as defined and illustrated by the Wurzburg school. See the works of Watt, Messer, and Bühler.

[7] I defined lyricism above (chapter 1) as a "specific double capacity of expansion and integration" as "an imperative to exaltation." Following this proposition, the word *tendentious* seems to me to be the most exact synonym of the term *lyrical.*

32

pothesis assumes that, to go from an image containing the ideogram to another image also containing it, there is always one and only one associative series. Now, it could be that there are several of them or that there are none at all, and in both cases the association would be made impossible through an excess or a lack of associative elements.

Other considerations come into play at this point. It is certainly far from inconceivable that there are several possible associative series between one principal element and another: for example, between van Dine's *The Bishop Murder Case* and "Antinea playing chess." Indeed, instead of the link being established via Pliny the Elder's and Flaubert's pessimism, another path, it seems, could just as well have been followed, such as, "The bow used to commit the crime with which *The Bishop Murder Case* begins, Artemis, Greek goddesses, Antinea the barbarian goddess."[8] It seems fairly difficult to appeal to a problematic economic principle in order to resolve this competition. There is nothing to prove that it is the shortest series that prevails. In any case, the most complete manifestations of lyrical thinking—deliriums and dreams—hardly suggest a bias toward avarice. One would do better to refer to the determinations that Thomas Brown pointed out in his posthumous text *Lessons on the Philosophy of the Human Mind:* the length and vividness of the original impression, the frequency and date of subsequent repetitions, the antagonism of the other associations, personality, habits, temperament, and so on. *They at least indicate that the real competition is between the secondary elements themselves: I will say between their respective emotional value and their latent systematization.*

---

[8] Contrary to appearances, this last association relies less on contrast than on contiguity. In fact the epigraph to Pierre Benoit's novel is as follows: "I have to warn you first of all before getting to the heart of the matter: do not be surprised to hear me call barbarians by Greek names." For a long time now I have been sensitive to this banal saying from the *Critias,* which seems to be very characteristic of that superior, distant atmosphere of Plato's dialogues.

The other case to be examined turns our attention to essentially the same question. What, in fact, can happen when the cyclical power of an ideogram is exhausted, when the elements containing it and possessing an appreciable affective value have already been evoked? This is apparently the only case when the constitution of an associative series is impossible, *for in a continuous experience there is by definition a path that, however long it is, can join together any two representations contiguously, just as in a united and coherent world there is by definition one that can join them together by resemblance,* or, to use a word that has taken on a more precise meaning — *by correspondence.*[9] On the contrary, the ideogram fairly soon runs out of representations capable of making it appear in all its brilliance, for it is rare for it to have been present in a large number of deep emotions. The richness of the chess game is already exceptional for me. What happens, then, when the powerful images have already been evoked and only the indifferent or almost indifferent ones are left? *It seems that at this point, when the lyrical power of the ideogram has, so to speak, lost its charge, it is the most moving of the secondary representations, having been used to induce the ideogram the last time, that takes command of the association and reorients it toward its own crystallization.*

Thus, either case — of an overabundance or of a shortage of associative possibilities — is suitable for considering the secondary representations in and of themselves, which until now have been viewed only in relation to the principal representations. Perhaps they, too, are not as independent as they at first appear to be.

---

[9] See B. Pascal, *Pensées,* ed. Brunschvicg, vol. 1, pp. 32-33; E. Swedenborg, *Arcana Coelestia,* passim; Charles Baudelaire, *The Flowers of Evil,* "Spleen and Ideal IV." This term at least has the advantage of allowing those associations that result from an *affective identity* to be included among the associations by resemblance, because they are not the least numerous.

II. IDEOGRAMMATIC THEMES

There is no doubt that the "chess delirium" formed itself thanks to the power of absorption of this ideogram, but if it is true that the world of mental images is submitted to a multiple systematization, the elements absorbed do not have to be indifferent to one another. In fact, the intermediary representations evoked appear to belong to three main affective themes, to mention only the immediate intersections (and I would not have any of the other ones intervene so as not to leave myself open to the reproach of using facts too much to suit my own argument).[1]

First of all, some themes contain a demoralizing aspect that affects me in quite a remarkable manner and that seems to me to be due to a pessimistic attitude that has reached its limit, this limit being, in my opinion, the absolute lack of any exaltation with regard to this attitude. The theme of depreciation is illustrated thus in the evocation of Riemann-Christoffel's formula that, like all the data of mathematical physics and stellar astronomy, effectively contributes to the total discredit of humanity by turning it, in a sense, into an organism out of proportion to the true measure of things. A similarly belittling result is obtained by histological biology and in general by the thesis of the constitution of matter that, in breaking humans into molecules, atoms, and electrons, also contributes to depriving them of any kind of interest. Whence the evocation of van Dine's formula about humans as a "little hydrocarbonated animalcule." Such conceptions, both grandiose

---

[1] Such a reproach can only be understood, moreover, with reference to the hypothesis according to which theoretical thinking would have tendencies that automatic thinking would not know about, which is highly improbable because of the reciprocal determination that exists between the two.

and disappointing, seem to me to be, more than ever, salutary and—even more terrible than the famous passage from Pascal, "That is where natural knowledge leads us . . ."[2]—even more frightening and decisive than the tale in which Leonid Andreyev describes the apperception of the world of the omniscient Lazarus resurrected. These are not the least of the motives that incite me to study the natural sciences.

Once again it is the theme of pessimism that is concealed beneath the metion of *The Temptation of Saint Anthony.* For about six months I had been truly bothered (and I did not hesitate to expound on this problem to my friends) by the thought that one and the same man, Flaubert—whose personality I have no desire to explore any further, and the author of several works about which I can say, at the very least, I see nothing to get out of them—was able to write two books as opposite in technique and inspiration and as profoundly moving and hypocritical (in the best sense of the term) as *The Temptation of Saint Anthony* and *A Sentimental Education.* Considered in this light, it appears that the evocation of the one is only there in order to cover up that of the other.[3] This book that, ever since I read it, I had continually praised as the novel capable of producing the most mediocre despair, the most complete prostration, the only one whose hero one is not tempted to identify with, in a word, the most debilitating and demoralizing book there is—I was forced to discover this in the course of the analysis—I had altogether too many reasons to fear.

The second of the themes that can be divined through the "chess delirium" is that of the femme fatale. It formed itself entirely around the character of Antinea. I read the novel *Atlantida* when I was very

---

[2] B. Pascal, *Pensées,* ed. Brunschvicg, vol. 2, p. 72.

[3] I refer here to the notion of a "screen memory" as defined in the works of psychoanalysis.

young, and it is a work whose mythological significance still appears to me to be on the one hand particularly serious and on the other hand totally independent of Mr. Pierre Benoit's personality.[4] I was outraged that everyone wanted to make Antinea the allegorical personification of the allegedly dangerous attraction of the desert, an interpretation reinforced by my mother because one of her girlfriends had abandoned her husband and children to return to the Sahara, where, during a trip practically all on her own, she already ventured far. I was planning to write a very somber "Essay on the concept of the femme fatale." For me the actress Brigitte Helm, whom I had seen for the first time in the film *Metropolis*—which is itself not a matter of indifference, from several points of view—seemed to me a perfect illustration of those emphatic creatures. I considered it entirely appropriate that Pabst had chosen her to incarnate this illusory and disarming heroine of *Atlantida,* and for me this choice took on the value of a public vindication, if not a personal victory. The evocation of Mona, whom I got to know more intimately about that time, is part of the same theme, for beside the fact that I quickly considered her a femme fatale—a condensation that her very noble bearing would certainly have made possible were it not constantly belied by her pitiful and vulgar behavior, but one that was above all determined by my theoretical preoccupations concerning the true significance of the concept of a femme fatale—I had had more particularly identified her with Antinea. This was not only because of the resemblance that I believed existed between her and Briggitte Helm, a resemblance that in the associative chain would allow me to pass from the one to the other, but also because of the quite independent fact that

---

[4] See infra. "Supporting and Supplementary Documents," pp. 121-124.

I had accompanied her to the Miracles cinema: she was going to book seats for that very evening with her husband, precisely to attend a screening of the film *Atlantida* with Brigitte Helm in the role of Antinea.

A third and final theme would be that of the cruel female sovereign. It intervenes explicitly through the evocation of Catherine of Russia, whom Sacher-Masoch associates just as admiringly with the merciless and little-known queens he usually chooses as the heroines of his tales, and who also, in the story he adapts, has the automaton chess player shot on a whim and more than on a whim. A's ultimate intervention is closely linked to this theme: indeed, the most recent conversation I had had with her was precisely about masochism. Even more recently in a letter addressed to me in Poland she had made a confession, in answer to my question concerning the cruelty of deeply masochistic instincts. She told me about it in these terms:

> *in particular, troubled dreams which began before I fell asleep, since my childhood and becoming more and more vivid over time. The theme: a very cruel woman who was cruel to everyone until she met the person who loved her cruelly, and whom she loved for that very reason; above all physical cruelty. Not only does she accept this, but she derives great enjoyment from it, not really understanding love any other way. These dreams, pursued complacently when awake, betray a deep desire: to suffer the cruelty of the person one loves. (To be the vampire's prey.) The masochistic tendency is the deepest one, but inversely, with respect to the loved one, the cruelty is paralyzed except if it is someone of the same sex (at least with lesbianism). Which is to me quite natural and leads me to think that one of the ends of cruelty is to penetrate, with the greatest possible enjoyment and via these supernatural means, what it is one loves. To devour the loved object. Without any Christian inversion, moreover (which confirms self-cruelty), since*

it is allied on the contrary to the love of one's body; one
does not possess oneself by narcissistic contemplation.
(August 31, 1933)

This very unexpected confession nonetheless corroborated a commentary she had given at my request on the photograph reproduced in
the first issue of *Le Surréalisme au service de la révolution [Surrealism*
in the Service of the Revolution] and has as its title these words, which
are more significant than they seem: "Sometimes on Sundays . . ."[5] It
shows, in the most desirable of prosaically bourgeois drawings rooms,
with a hint of poetry in it, a young girl lying on the couch, her eyes
wide open and distracted, and to whom A had, as expected, attributed
her own desires in her interpretation:

> *Sometimes on Sundays, she gives herself up to caresses*
> *that exceed all reality; her arm falling, her body passive*
> *yet eager, waiting for the wild embrace that her ecstatic*
> *eyes are imagining. Like the thirst of a martyr. . . .*
> *Making her genitals quiver until they hurt, her hand not*
> *arousing them, or at least not consciously—her conscious-*
> *ness is totally absorbed by them. In return, they arouse in*
> *her eyes and in her mouth those mad desires for a land*
> *where men love desperately, and kill what they love. Kill*
> *with a cruelty that makes all of her limbs stir voluptuously*
> *—crushed without a gesture, her body thoroughly pene-*
> *trated, her blood drunk, and in his veins, coming out of*
> *her heart, and a desire to at last feel dead, beheaded, like a*
> *vampire's prey.*

---

[5] Taken from the film by Luis Bunuel and
Salvador Dali, *L'Age d'or [The Golden*
Age].

The obsession with vampirism aside, in which I could feel particularly targeted, the special prominence given by my friend to cruelty considerably enriched, by contrast, my ambivalent interest in the royal women described so lyrically by Leopold von Sacher-Masoch that led me to identify, in an article I wrote at the time, a thin plaster model made by Alberto Giacometti with the feminine automaton fitted with razor blades, "the magnificent steel woman," "the metal beauty," used by one of these women in the tale entitled "The Water of Youth" to torture her lover.

Those are the three principal ideogrammatic themes that show through the woven texture of the "chess delirium." *Thus the secondary elements not only serve to connect and, to a certain extent, to qualify the principal elements containing the dominant ideogram, but in turn themselves form determined series as a kind of infrastructure.* In addition, these series are not autonomous; on the contrary, they have both deep affective affinities between themselves, which do not belong to their content, and accidental intersections, which are a product of my own experience.

Indeed, the theme of human depreciation is closely related to that of the femme fatale, of which it is, so to speak, a particular instance: man's humiliation before a woman childishly considered more as a giant, as a natural force, an inflexible element possessing its own laws and sticking to them. The parallel has its concrete expression in the "chess delirium," in which on the one hand Mona and Antinea are evoked who both imply the presence of the femme fatale, and on the other, secretly but indisputably, the terrible and hopeless *Sentimental Education*. Now, the effect this work had on me would not have been so acute if my adventure with Mona had not so incredibly resembled the beginning of Frederic Moreau's with Madame Arnould, if only because of the already more-than-sufficient fact that Mona was already a married woman, from a higher social class than mine, first caught sight of in the provinces and found again shortly afterward in Paris.

The intermediary of the chess game was not strictly necessary in order to get from the theme of total demoralization to that of the femme fatale: they determine each other reciprocally. The same is true of the theme of the femme fatale and that of the cruel queen: they are so closely connected that one wonders whether their distinction is not arbitrary. In addition to this potential identity, would one not have to point out that the character of Antinea is precisely both that of a femme fatale and that of a distant and merciless sovereign? This conjunction is rarer than one would think. She is the only character of all those who have been considered up until now part of both one and the other; for Catherine the Great cannot be taken for a femme fatale, and neither can Brigitte Helm, a quiet housewife in real life (so they say) be taken for a cruel queen.

Moreover, *The Temptation of Saint Anthony,* expressly evoked in the "chess delirium," contains a number of allusions to the previous themes and contributes to overdetermining them still further in relations to one another.

Appearing as the story of a failure (*échec*), *The Temptation of Saint Anthony* is associated consciously with Antinea's failure with Captain Morhange and at the same time unconsciously with the theme of successive failures, with the irresistible decline that is the subject of *Sentimental Education* (a work written precisely, and incomprehensibly, by the same author), and with the central ideogram: the game of chess (*le jeu des échecs*). Finally, to cap it all, the only sentence I remember from *The Temptation of Saint Anthony* is the following: "I know the secret of the tombs where the old kings sleep. A chain coming out from the wall holds their heads up. Nearby, in a pool of porphyry, women they have loved float on black liquids.[6] Now, this sentence seems to me

---

[6] G. Flaubert, *The Temptation of Saint Anthony,* chapter 7.

more and more to be exactly, mysteriously, and obviously symmetrical to the central myth of Atlantida as exemplified by another sentence that, likewise, is the one from Pierre Benoit's novel I found the most striking: "Your brothers in love, the fifty knights of orichalch, await you, mute and grave, in the red marble hall."[7]

Let us now turn to the associative chain of the chess game: No element remains that could not be related to multipolar ways to all of the others. The principal representations and the secondary representations are just as overdetermined among themselves as they are in relation to one another. The emblematic and passional image of the chess game binds together this astonishing coherence. Not only does it maintain, with each element, the episodic and contingent relation used in the series of associations, but hidden links bind it to the secondary themes: thus the appellation "game of *chess*" ("jeu des *échecs*," play of *checks* or *failures*) is not indifferent to the demonstration; and thus the fact that the most powerful piece of the game is called the *queen* is not without importance for the other two.

This doubtlessly incomplete analysis of a very ordinary automatic association of ideas—the first one that *came along,* to be precise—could be taken as an exemplary probe into the world of the mind. It brings to light two important results: *the remarkable interdependence of representations and the infinite complexity of their reciprocal overdetermination, and the extraordinary power of annexation and systematization of passions in lyrical ideograms.*

---

[7] Pierre Benoit, *Atlantida*, trans. Mary C. Tongue and Mary Ross (New York: Duffield and Company, 1920), p. 300. Rereading *The Temptation of Saint Anthony,* I discovered not far from the sentence quoted above an explicit allusion to Atlantida, the Chimera who says that it is she who "surrounded the harbors of Atlantida with a wall of orichalch," which further overdetermines the association. (What is more, this second reading brought to light other overdeterminations. See the footnote in chapter V where the objective lyrical value of the praying mantis is studied; this constitutes a real and concrete condensation of the ideogrammatic themes that are envisaged here subjectively.)

IV

THE SYNTHESES OF LYRICAL THINKING

The study of the associative chain of the chess game allowed the substance and, in a sense, the hypothesis of lyrical thinking to be brought to the fore: the multiple overdetermination of conscious representations with respect to one another. I was thus led to conclude that, far from demonstrating the arbitrariness of the mind, each association merely revealed a rigorous necessity, for the irreducible singularity of each element (within which is also inherent the equally irreducible singularity of its connections to the other elements) is precisely that by which it is forced to play the singular role in a given singular association, which it alone can perform to the exclusion of the other elements.

It has to be said once and for all: If the philosophers who have studied the association of ideas had not done it artificially, asking themselves in the abstract why the inductive element is associated with a unique induced element, when many other inducible elements bear such suggestive resemblances with, or are so closely contiguous to, this inductive element—whether, if they had instead considered the concrete multiplicity of the relations of the particular elements that are actually associated, they would have noticed that nothing is ever associated with just anything, but each term with the one it must associate with.[1]

---

[1] See infra, "Supporting and Supplementary Documents," III, pp. 125-128

43

Automatic thinking is thus possible only because of a general overdetermination of elements. But this is only, in a sense, a plasma that requires an ordering activity: precisely that of the lyrical ideogram. When set up, an associative chain lends itself to analysis and uncovers *its conditions of possibility* and *the mechanism of its necessity*. It is nonetheless true that it is the result of a synthetic function that joins together the disparate elements, and that is the determining emotional power itself. It is the presence of an ideogram alone that allows the associations of automatic thinking to be analyzed. Otherwise, they ensure their connection themselves, which is to say that none of the terms joined together is contained in any of the others or already related to it because of a former association. We are dealing here, therefore, with actual syntheses of images, or of metaphors—how we name them is of no importance—that are performed by the lyrical process and help to create, for their own use and to their own ends, *relationships* intended to link together the opposing affective themes and, if need be (as in dreams, and perhaps outside of them), the *representations* that fuse them together.[2]

It seems appropriate in this respect to look at an ordinary lyrical text. I will take the most recent one I have written (which is nevertheless almost ten years old), "The Navigators' Poem":

> *They had trouble separating themselves from the void,*
> *mythology had no charm for them, a hollow thing on the*
> *plateau with their parabolic reflecting bodies, with space,*
> *the lawn for the lunatics in the asylum, the pine tree of*

---

[2] I also think that the affective imagination alone, because of the imperative to annexation and proliferation that characterizes the lyrical process, possesses a synthetic power. Indeed, synthetic judgments are dependent on or independent from experience, that is, a priori or a posteriori. Now, in the latter case, empirical syntheses—those of perception—are easily reducible to analysis; one soon notices that the judgment involved consists of drawing out, from an undifferentiated set of associations, certain qualities whose association is asserted. As for the alleged a priori judgments (a straight line is the shortest route between two points,

*irreproachable dynasties—Augurs of themselves. They
delighted in symmetrical and terrible meditations such as
the game of dice (their faces diversely punctuated, space
upon space).*

At first glance nothing could give a more absolute impression of
discontinuity, nothing could be less like the association of the chess
game, where all the terms fitted into each other by way of a sort of
common denominator: the scientific pessimism that linked van Dine's
novel to Pliny the Elder, the same supernatural elements joining the
latter to Flaubert, and so on. The connection was always made by what
formal logic calls a middle term, in this case a link of resemblance or
of contiguity. Moreover, because of the cyclical return of the ideogram,
the associative chain did have a kind of subject. In the present text there
is nothing of the sort: there is neither a subject nor any apparent
relation. In contradistinction to the automatic association of ideas, lyrical thinking is synthetic: thus the determination and the overdetermination of the elements remain hidden; but they are no less present and
effective for all that.

I have to mention, first of all, that these few lines I called, for the
sake of convenience, "The Navigators' Poem" clearly bear the mark of
my preoccupation at the time with the relationship among personality,
body, and space that had surfaced in the course of psychasthenic symptoms, which I had tried to aggravate to an extreme degree (with some
success, I might add), especially during those interminable moments
when I would try in vain to go to sleep. I will subsequently present a

---

etc.), these are, properly speaking, analyses of the mind operating on the unity
of its pure intuition and extracting from
it certain *transcendental, indissoluble
properties,* whose terms are identified after the fact. In both cases the synthesis is
given beforehand: a passivity on which
understanding exerts its analytic activity.

certain number of documents that will attest to the way in which I had used this propensity for explicitly ascetic ends in terms both of sensation and of interpretation. In the "poem" quoted above, expressions such as "trouble separating themselves from the void," "a hollow thing on the plateau with their parabolic bodies," and "space upon space" undeniably relate to these attempts at metamorphosis, which will become clear if one refers to the introspective descriptions quoted in one of the following chapters and written at about the same time.

When light is shed on the origin and the essential determination of "The Navigators' Poem," it begins to take on a certain affective continuity. It is also possible (despite their temporal difference) to find in it two secondary ideogrammatic themes: that of the dice and that of the dynasty.

Concerning the dice, it is important to mention (for want of more extensive research, a simple sketch being sufficient for now) the principal fact governing their evocation. Besides their objective emblematic value, which makes them the most common representation of fate (that is, the distressing image of the circumstances on which people depend and that do not depend on them), the dice assumed a more concrete significance for me. At the time I would always carry two with me and indulge in simple exercises of calculating the probability of their two faces ("diversely punctuated," as I wrote in the "poem") coming up the same. This was a half-mechanical, half-voluntary artifice that I used in order both to conceal and to express a recent painful experience having to do with the possibilities of agreement between two beings, and in order to console myself hypocritically for this failure with the help of statistical considerations, a sordid kind of consolation that, had it been presented in a direct and obvious manner, my exacerbated sensibility would have taken very badly at the time.

The other theme, the one that appears in the word *dynasty,* is linked to formulas I still remember very clearly. The epithet *irreproachable* to which it is attached is an allusion, even more than to the dynasties of ancient Egypt that, nonetheless, have great evocative value, to the astonishing and at certain times secularized Romanov dynasty, that long succession of emperors who, if they were crazy, were no less the sovereigns (by definition autocratic and orthodox to the highest degree) on whom the immense and wonderful Northern regions, the most lethargic countries on earth, were greatly dependent. I was especially interested in that eminently unhappy man, the Tsar Paul I. I had carefully read a huge book about his childhood. It had been a warning that had always struck me, because, coming from a man who was so unaware of the very existence of the problems that I liked to contemplate, his lucidity and precision were disturbing: "So you want to know how a prince who went mad was raised?" But the concept of a dynasty, with its evocation of an absolute power entrusted by a totally irrational principle to the hands of someone who could only make very dangerous use of it, really did not worry me that much, although because of this it also became part of my disproportionate lyrical interest in cruel queens. I was above all attached to the notion that it particularly illustrates—of unchanging, immemorial, primeval historical lineage—an attraction that was so unrelated to the rest of my moods that it seemed to invite a search for a psychoanalytic explanation. Such an explanation would, for example, point to the analogous contradiction opposing the reflections of the ego worried about its origin and its right, and the fact, quite unwarranted in all fairness, of corporeal existence that, although it is ultimately the origin of this right, loses itself in the unconscious life of the womb in the same way that the only claim to legitimacy of a dynasty is to descend from the *mists of time.*

Finally, it will be worthwhile to quote, in order to clarify the quite special way in which I understood the notion of a dynasty, a few lines I scribbled on paper following a disappointment I suffered in relation to an unknown young woman seated across from me in a railway compartment, who, when her eyes were closed, had held my attention by the motionlessness and great nobility of her face, but who quickly erased the impression of eternal life that emanated from it by the extremely vulgar way in which she powdered it—a gesture that I insist should be executed in an exultant and perfect, almost ritual manner, knowing full well from experience the quality of emotion it usually serves to conceal:

> *She had a secular face which already confirmed her as*
> *the continuation of a long dynasty, the latest descendent of*
> *a legendary hero, when with a rapid gesture she destroyed*
> *the ancient sleep of her face: she was a hollow being, with-*
> *out origin, a slight error of the goodwill of the others.*

This short notation reveals quite well the preoccupation latent within the theme of the dynasty: the desire to place one's own existence above all justification, which implies the fear of thereby committing oneself to an intrauterine consciousness that is all too identifiable with sleep, if not death.

This analysis brings to an end what can be determined with any certainty. Indeed, the overdetermination of the other elements that make up "The Navigators' Poem" eludes me for the most part, so that I now have to enter the generally dissatisfying realm of probabilities, or perhaps it would be better to say the realm of ignorance pure and simple. Whatever the case may be, I ought first to stress the term *pine tree,* which is very closely linked to the "dynasty" theme that has just been examined. I do not think that we are here dealing with the evocation of some family tree. It is far more likely that it is a reminiscence of the 1868 postage stamp from the South African republic of Orange representing a tree flanked by three horns, which is, of course, an orange tree that I had always mistaken for a pine tree. Now, Prince William of *Orange,* known as William the Silent, the man who took the energy of despair to such extremes as to assert that it is not necessary to hope in order to undertake nor to suceed in order to persevere, had always seemed to me to be one of the most dynastic of figures, in the special sense of the word. I mentioned him several times in this way when I was writing the text here in question; that is, the expression "the pine tree of irreproachable dynasties" would in fact be a synthetic association based on the latent evocation of the Silent One; it will not appear entirely arbitrary (if only because of the nickname) to assume this evocation to be overdetermined by the central theme of psychasthenia.

It seems that a similar overdetermination governed the intervention of the "lawn for the lunatics in the asylum." During my analysis this element provoked a hypermnesic image, which I identified after some effort as being that of the lawn of a hospital in Reims where, as a child, I had gone with my parents to visit a great-aunt who was undergoing some operation. Because the visit seemed to be dragging on, I had gone down to the lawn to play. It was certainly not an insane asylum, but a year later, when this relative died, I learned that since the disappearance of her son in the war, she had been intensely involved in spiritualism, which made my parents classify her as a half-crazy woman. This made a strong impression on me, however, and I insisted they give me the innumerable sheets of paper she had covered with mediumistic writing. I nonetheless found them extremely disappointing to read.

This would not in and of itself have been enought to make my unconscious transform the hospital where she had been treated into an insane asylum, had the way for this confusion not been paved over a long time. In fact, when I was about three or four years old (these are my oldest memories), I lived in Saint-Maurice, in a suburb just to the west of Paris. I could only just distinguish, as I should have been able to do, among three buildings I conflated out of a feeling of fear. All were referred to as asylums: the kindergarten, where they were starting to take me and where men in white coats, under the pretext of disinfecting the place, had once, to my unutterable and lasting horror, handled instruments that were strange, to say the least; the home for the disabled (it was during the war), where every day I could see amputees, who did not fail to make a strong impression on me; and, most of all, the Charenton insane asylum, as it was called, whose gardens and lawns I saw during walks on Sundays, and where, if I misbehaved, they threatened to lock me up and leave me to the mercy of the terrible figures in white coats mentioned above. What is more, about the time I had gone to see my great-aunt at the hospital in Reims I had also returned to this very same insane asylum, which had by then been converted into a maternity hospital; my mother's sister-in-law had just given birth there. I arrived very excited at the thought of perhaps having some light shed on the mystery of birth, being at the time so ignorant of everything concerned with generation and sexuality that it did not even occur to me—despite being about fourteen years old—that a woman could be anatomically different from a man. The confusion of these memories is all the more explicable because, apart from the similarity of the visits, there is the fact that I called both of the two women patients "my aunt" without differentiating, despite their being different relatives, which I was incapable of really understanding.

More recently, since I moved to Vitry-sur-Seine, a new element has intervened that has helped make the preceding elements into an indissoluble affective totality. This is a lawn that I see several times a day as I go past it in the train on my way to or from Paris. It is oddly bordered with trees grouped in such a way to form exits on different levels as the lawn recedes, like the wings of a stage-set in the theater. At the end of the lawn is a house whose windows are always closed, which appears quite peculiar because of an immense open porch with double doors that looks out onto another lawn that is visible from the green at the back. The landscape is always deserted, and it looks as if it was meant to be that way. One time, however, I saw two human figures wearing white overblouses sitting on a stone bench located next to the tracks. With doleful eyes they were watching the trains go by, which led me to assume that I was in the presence of an insane asylum. But to this day I have no proof that this is the case. At any rate, nothing has ever given me the impression of something masked as much as does this lawn, isolated as if by miracle in one of the most populated urban agglomerations of Paris. Yet, despite my daily efforts, I have never been able to discover the least suspect detail in it that resembled a disguise or brought one to mind.

One can see the multiplicity of representations that concur to give the apparently quite neutral image of the "lawn for the insane in the asylum" a lyrical power that is due less to the number of possible associations than to the analogy and coherence of the memories it contains, and from which it draws its emotional effectiveness without any appreciable loss. The fact remains, nonetheless, that it is linked to the determining theme of the intellectual practice of psychasthenia only in a way that is quite superficial and as uncompromising as possible. Inversely, elements such as "augurs of themselves" and "reflecting" will appear very profoundly determined to those who have some experience of psychasthenic hyperconsciousness, by this particular brand of asceticism of the senses and of the mind. Yet I can still find no precise link to the slightest personal emotion: I have to take them in the most abstract manner, that is, with the extremely poor content one has to attribute to a word in order to use it.

Thus, in "The Navigators' Poem," we do in fact come across an overdetermining passional theme as well as secondary themes, themes such as that of the dice evoking humanity's fate and its inability not to be their victim (which is also the inability of the mind to preserve itself from discontinuity), or that of the dynasty covering up the terror of the precariousness of a consciousness faced with its intrauterine origin, its extinction in death, and its interruptions by sleep. These themes are really tied to the central preoccupations, but within them are also elements that either *are determined by a sufficient number of emotions, but are only very loosely connected to the essential inspiration* or *are very closely dependent on it, but are deprived of any concrete affective or mythogenic power.*

In short, however little one takes into account the failures of memory and the shortcomings of the analysis, none of these shortcomings compels us to assume an arbitrary power of the mind. One ought to feel instead that the elements whose genealogy I was unable to find failed me only because they never inspired a lasting or creative interest in me, and that the relationships, whose raison d'être escapes me for the time being—they are only justified in an extremely mediocre and really quite indifferent manner—were quickly elminated by others whose necessity was more immediate or deeper. In either case one can legitimately assert that *it is the lack of stimulating overdeterminations that limits the scope and value of such associations.* Now, I am mistrustful, to say the least, of the kind of activity that produces texts that, even written by me, are not entirely capable, to my mind, of justifying the elements that make them up, and that force me to consider the relationships according to which they present these elements as ill founded. It is clear that a text written in the same way by someone unknown to me is very likely to affect me just as much, that is to say, just as little.

This brings me to a difficulty that should have been taken into consideration more often: I am thinking of the problem posed on the one hand by the publication and on the other by the reading of poetic texts. For if these texts ultimately have their origin in the most personal, most intimate, and least communicable sources, it would seem that one ought neither to publish them nor to read them with the ambitious intentions generally exhibited by the very people who have great reservations about the possible extent of aesthetic pleasure. Not that these people are beyond using poetry as a pastime and, if need be, as a drug—that is, whenever I need to recite lines of poetry, in front of a mirror or not, if I am so poor as to be unable to procure for myself a more well-suited oblivion or enchantment through alcohol — but they retain enough good faith and lucidity to restrict, as is fitting, its theoretical value and to denounce, as is imperative, its moral mediocrity.

It is nonetheless true that with poetry, although refraining from dealing just with sensations (not to mention rhythm and music), one is putting one's money on both the objective and the subjective, and whatever reservations one might have as to the supreme value of such a distinction (and I for one never fail to have them), it is difficult not to recognize, particularly in the area of communication between minds, that it can boast an unquestionable practical importance. What is more, it does not seem to me that such an attitude, which consists in paying it no attention, is illegitimate in the present instance: I am even prepared to commend it, provided that one realizes the difficulty of the position and looks for the means of resolving the antinomy. Perhaps this resolution is quite simple: indeed, to the precise extent that the evolution of poetry has brought it closer and closer to an automatic activity and consequently has taken it further and further away from understanding as well as from the control of directed thinking and from the writer's clear consciousness, writers have fewer and fewer privileges over their readers when faced with their own work, which can appear to them to be, in extreme cases, as unfamiliar and uninterpretable as the work of a stranger. If the relationships had been knotted together with only the very slightest negligence, and had, so to speak, *insufficient funds* for the demands of a rigorous affective determinism, one could reproach writers neither for refusing to set the least store by such determinism nor for having to accept, if need be, the happy synthesis of an unknown imagination, which would aggravate the lyrical systematization of their obsessional ideograms.

Furthermore, this kind of borrowing seems inevitable if, as I have been led to believe, the systems of overdetermination also exist objectively. It follows mathematically, from the very fact that a relationship is insufficiently determined for one consciousness (whether or not it is the consciousness that has foregrounded this relationship by expressing it), that it is more than sufficiently determined for another one. It is useful at this point to make a comparison — according to the hypothesis just now recalled, a comparison is always an argument — with Leibniz's theory, which states that every monad is a reflection of the whole universe, but in occupying a particular place in this universe has a quite original and in no way interchangeable apperception of it, such that all of these apperceptions of the universe, these slightly but irreducibly different points of view, fit together and, far from being useless for one another, mutually complement each other with a properly infinite precision.

To return, after these reflections, to the "chess delirium," we would assert that one of the most moving associations and perhaps the one with the richest of consequences is not the fact of the synthetic activity of my own lyrical determinism, but that of a German film director's imagination, someone in whom I have absolutely no interest and for whom this association doubtless had merely an episodic value. It is nonetheless remarkable that the association of the chess game with the myth of Atlantida was made by someone other than myself, who had so many reasons to make it and for whom it was soon to receive a striking, personal verification: Mona, already identified moreover with

Antinea, quite unexpectedly knocking over all the chess pieces during a game in which she was what we were unavowedly playing for, just as the female sovereign of Atlantida is herself at stake in the game that she condescends to play with the distraught and trembling prisoner.

One can easily understand that I feel much more disoriented when faced with "The Navigators' Poem" written by me than when faced with the synthesis performed by the imagination of a man whose activity I am far from valuing; yet this is a necessary, moving, lyrical synthesis with which I feel immediately comfortable (do not forget that I am not that comfortable with life) and responds so well to the requirements of the passional themes that allow me only very little freedom, that it appears truly providential. *So the thesis of objective overdetermination is that of systematic providence.*

Thus, the existence of objective ideograms is implied, that is, objects that are so obviously signs that it becomes difficult for anyone not to be moved by their presence or their representation. Judging for example by the way in which writers, women, sorcerers, children, madmen, and doctors behave with mirrors, it does seem that these objects

---

[3] It would be necessary to write a study on the *phenomenology of the perception of virtual space with the help of mirrors and reflecting surfaces,* in which the question would be considered according to its main categories: optics, physiology, psychology, sociology, and mythology.

[4] Personal adventures should not only be understood as precise facts such as those that occupy a significant position in the "chess delirium," but also as affective attitudes, developments, or overdeterminations that have ripened in the unconscious and that it is the task of psychoanalytic technique to account for. Thus, the sexual pervert analyzed by R. de Sauddure (*Revue Française de Psychanalyse,* vol. 3, pp. 631-689. See also "Supporting and Supplementary Documents," II, p. 121) unexpectedly uses the chess game to express his castration anxiety: "A hippopotamus bites off my prick, spits it out again and vomits on it to defile it. I pick it up again and screw it back on. It's like in chess when you screw the knight back onto his horse."

possess in and of themselves an emotional and consequently a demonstrative power.[3] Is this not also true, although to a lesser degree, of the game of chess? The names of the pieces are not indifferent, in fact far from it, and neither are the alternating black and white squares on the chessboard; nor the number of possible combinations, which is far greater even than that expressed by the sum of the grains of wheat placed in geometrical progression and doubled on each of the sixty-four squares; nor the perfect elimination of chance; nor the perfidiousness of certain moves such as double check and discovered check. These determinations are universally valid, and everyone can add personal adventures such that, however slight one's familiarity with the few works in which the game of chess plays an appreciable role and, like van Dine's novel or the story of Kempelen's automaton, connects it to sentiments, which everything leads us to believe should be felt as the theme of scientific pessimism, or of the femme fatale.[4] The emotional and mythically objective value of the game of chess is thereby established and thus assigned a monopolizing and systematizing power over the other representations.

From the point of view of the appropriateness of the comparison, nothing holds together: a) The knight is not made up of a horse and a knight, but the bust of a horse and its support. In the very rare games in which the piece is represented by a horse and its knight, the two elements are of a piece, and it is consequently impossible for them to be disconnected. b) One does not screw on, one puts on or slips on the top part. c) The two elements are more or less the same size. They are much less assimilable to a man and his genitals than to a man and a woman coupled together, or to their genitals taken separately. So I think that the image in question refers to castration only through a screen mechanism, and that in fact it is an allusion to coitus.

It is also common knowledge that many obscene metaphors for intercourse are borrowed from the vocabulary of horse-riding.

In the same perspective I should, for my part, include the fact that the game of chess is for me very closely linked to the development of the Oedipus complex. I was very young when my father taught me this game, and in time I managed to turn the tables on him and to beat him almost every time. There is no doubt that the disproportionate interest I took in these defeats or these victories points to more obscure conflicts.

We can thus understand why certain ideas, images, or objects exert a dominant attraction over the imagination and why in particular they are used more than average in lyrical modes of expression. The findings of psychoanalysis appear eminently capable of determining these privileged representations, and analysts have not failed to discover a large number of them, but they have perhaps not been quite so inspired in considering them a bit hastily as symbols. Whatever the case may be, we can better understand why a poetic text may be usable; it is necessarily very rare that it not contain one or more of these ideograms laden with meaning that have something in them for everyone.

So I had no reason to be surprised that some unknown person should have connected up, as it was important for me to do and as the circumstances made sure of doing for me before my very eyes, the game of chess with the queen of Atlantida or her substitutes. This is not so much a coincidence as a confirmation. More generally speaking, I ought not to be surprised that, independently of any socially based mimesis, the same elements interest people who might otherwise have little in common: the reason being that everyone can attach to them associations whose affective quality, not to say quantity, is always exceptional.

In this perspective, the fact that last year René Char, one of the authors of *Ralentir Travaux (Slow Down Construction),* pointed out to me as the two lines of poetry that had most moved him precisely those that had by far made the greatest impression on me, has nothing unusual about it, as I discovered when I analyzed them.[5] These lines, from the last poem in the collction, are as follows:

---

[5] See André Breton, René Char, Paul Eluard: *Ralentir Travaux,* Editions Surréalistes, 1930.

The women who in love hear the wind pass through the
    poplar trees
The women who in hate are more taut than praying
    mantises.

A synthetic relationship is clearly established in these lines, in which the copulas are moreover extremely loose. Indeed, if from the preliminary perspective of verisimilitude "hear" and "taut" cause few problems, and even if one can justify them to a large extent (the sense of hearing seems to be the best way of perceiving the wind, and "taut" *[elancé]* seems to be one of those rare, very precise adjectives that can apply both to hatred and to praying mantises, to love and to poplar trees), one has to admit that they are so vague and so general that they cannot claim—just in exceptional circumstances—to evoke any particular concrete image. On the contrary, the contrast between, or the identity of, love and hatred, which is the cause of all ambivalence, awakens an expectation in everyone and puts everyone in a particular frame of mind, even when it does not evoke any well-determined adventure. So one can consider that the bringing together of these two words alone opens up an ideogrammatic theme that has universal value; that is, it provokes a state of mind highly favorable to the play of systematizing lyrical activity, even though in the present example the likely effect is in danger of being considerably dulled by habit, so banal, frequent, and worn out is the association.

What remains now is to study the mythical, objective, and subjective value of the concrete elements that intervene in the two lines from *Ralentir Travaux.*

First of all, the poplar tree is not just any term of comparison for me: it is, in fact, supported by very old memories that, if they are only in a very childish way associated with the pact with the devil, at least situate it in a very precise infernal atmosphere that has never ceased to be present in my imagination in its original form. This form is that of a sentimental ballad that was often sung to me, at my repeated request, by my paternal grandmother, whom I loved more than anyone else because she always took my side against my parents, with an almost wild energy defending my most unreasonable whims or satisfying them in secret. It was during the war in a marshy, wooded area of Champagne; I was about five years old and believed that I recognized the place where the legend had taken place, in a wood that I had entered alone at night, and I never failed to get my grandmother to show me the "black poplar trees," which I could find perfectly well. This sentimental ballad, which I will reproduce here in its entirety, was written with a vocabulary that is far too advanced for early childhood, as one can see.

"The Gold Crowns"

One evening down by the rill
Underneath the black poplar trees
Next to the miller's wife's mill
A six-foot-tall man passed by me:
His moustache was as grey as a mare
He wore a blue coat and trilby;
The North Wind blew, tousling his hair;
The Devil or Good Lord was he.
His voice resounded, loud and deep,
Like a great brass horn it did sound;
He said: "Follow me through the trees,
I'll give you a hundred gold crowns."

Without resisting I did follow,
Hypnotized by his deep red eye,
Had he led me to the gallows,
I would never have backed away:
He raced on faster than a hare
Without even seeming to hie;
I shook from fever and from fear
I thought I was going to die.
But so as then to revive me,
His voice resounding deep and loud,

Said: "Follow me into the trees
I'll give you a hundred gold crowns."

We reached the heart of the forest
The night was dark, and the green trees
Threw green flames high into the mist.
I thought we were in Hades.
A dreadful flash of lightning struck,
And disfigured the stranger's face:
I saw the devil, What a shock!
With his hornèd head and his tail;
He showed me a book, I'd no choice,
In which nothing was written down,
And asked me in his deep brass voice
"Do you want a hundred gold crowns?"

"Swear by your blood and soul to me,
Swear by the devil and the Lord,
That no woman will you marry
From this hamlet or from abroad,
At least not till you're two score gone,
And that we'll see you every day
From one girl to the next one run
With no single love holding sway."
When the book he'd reddened with his claw,
His voice in its deep brass sound
Said: "Sign and all this will be yours,
A hundred jingling gold crowns."

Instead of signing on the page
Which the devil's fingers had brushed
I thought that it would be more sage
To make a sign of the cross.
Up into smoke the devil went,
And I was then transported back,

To my dear miller's wife was sent.
In a room full of flour sacks
She said: "Here, I will give to you
My heart, my mill, all that I own."
That fine woman gave me, O joy!
A hundred golden large brass crowns.

This story seemed all the more fantastic to me because I little understood the terms: the words *bise* ("North Wind"), *frayeur* ("fear"), *louis* ("crown"), *quarantaine* ("two score"), *fredaine* ("running from one girl to the next"), had only a vague and imprecise meaning for me, if they had any at all. I tried in vain to think of what could be meant by the two lines:

He raced on faster than a hare
Without even seeming to hie.

I imagined a six-foot man as a monster with six legs and not as a strapping individual who was two meters tall: I identified him more or less with the terrifying animal-like silhouette of the steamrollers that I had seen through the evening mist and whose headlamps when lit up seemed to me like two crossed eyes. I also did not think that a "sign of the cross" could be the quick gesture I was made to perform in the evening after prayer. As for the intervention of the miller's wife, which concludes the ballad, to the extent that I paid it the slightest bit of attention, it seemed to me the most incomprehensible thing of all. In any case, I was too frightened at that point to listen anymore, and I could only think of the terrible encounters that one can have, and that I had had, in the shade of certain types of large thin trees called poplars.

The memory of landscapes with poplar trees where I was so afraid of coming face to face with a man "with a grey moustache" or with the threatening form of a steamroller is certainly one of the memories that has affected me the most profoundly. One can understand even now why the word *poplar* awakens within me those distant terrors, about which psychoanalysis has shown that, even if they single out the wrong object, they nonetheless echo deeply solemn realities. It was no doubt while under this influence that two years ago I wrote the following lyrical text:

> *Beautiful women go by far off, in the rain. They are*
> *playing-cards. Women traveling at dawn, bathed in starry*
> *sheets of ice, cornered in evil, until insomnia.*
>
> *Women traveling at dawn, traveling at dusk, traveling in*
> *mourning, traveling at all hours, in silk capes and black*
> *gloves, in fields fertilized by the decomposition of a multi-*
> *tude of severed hands, and where only a few phallic poplar*
> *trees grow, flanked by giant metronomes, which solemnly*
> *but languidly keep love's time.*
>
> *Femmes fatales at dawn, women traveling or bathing,*
> *your looks fall, and the intervals of your looks, your plati-*
> *num eyelids. So beautiful as to inspire fear in the countries*
> *under low skies where everything casts great shadows, I*
> *would have acclaimed your clear contempt.*

It is worthwhile pointing out that these lines, as was to be ex-pected, link up the poplar trees to other ideograms already indicated in this study: particularly through the expression "femmes fatales at dawn," which needs no comment, and more interestingly, through the assertion that "they are playing-cards," which is doubly overdeter-mined. First, in relation to the chess game and to Mona: while I was playing against her husband (the outcome of which I have mentioned), she was having me choose cards, and I was telling her the stereotyped meaning that the most unskilled of fortune-tellers give them (spades means suffering, death; hearts means joy, love, etc.), which is also likely in its turn to be overdetermined. And second, in relation to the dice, which share with cards the power of representing emblematically our consent to be the most dependent upon that which least depends upon us, and for this reason I contrasted with the game of chess, where

the intervention of chance is indeed eliminated at the outset and theoretically at least in the course of the game.

But it is more important to observe, for my present concerns, that
in the text in question the poplar trees are associated, through the
intermediary of the "giant metronomes," with love, as they already
were in the lines from *Ralentir Travaux* and, although more loosely, in
the ballad "The Gold Crowns." One is thus led to believe that such an
association is more justified than it appears: The epithet *phallic,* which
is apposed to them and which André Breton, who wrote the image in
Ralentir Travaux, spontaneously gave to them later when I asked him
about it, shows by its precision that the poplar tree can indeed be
objectively (that is, irrespective of any personal contingency) associated
with love.[6]

It can now be seen that the association of the wind with poplar
trees is much deeper than the natural connection of the two would lead
us to suppose. The word *poplar* comes from the Latin *populare,* a
double form that some claim must be related to the Greek: $\pi\acute{\alpha}\lambda\lambda\omega$
from $\pi\acute{\epsilon}\pi\eta\lambda\alpha$, which designates a light and quick agitation: the poplar
tree is thus by definition the tree whose leaves are incessantly in mo-
tion, at the slightest breeze, which is unfailingly confirmed by experience. It is also known that there is a variety of poplar called the aspen
(*le tremble*), a word whose etymology is obviously analogous.

With the praying mantis the objective lyrical capacity of the ideogram takes on truly disturbing proportions. My interest in it is also no
less decisive. Being an insect collector, I was attracted to this particular
one at an early age, all the more so because at that time we lived in

---

[6] See infra, "Supporting and Supplementary Documents," IV, p. 129.

eastern France, where it is not found, and I had never seen one: the difficulty of getting a specimen only increased my desire to possess one. I had to wait two years, and finally during a summer vacation in Royan I was thrilled to capture a fine *Mantis religiosa*. Later on this catch became, in my memory, part of an indivisible series of adventures, in the humblest but also most compromising sense of the word. More and more, as the inevitably disappointing and monotonous years keep slipping away, these adventures seem to me to be an uninterrupted continuity of inimitable and, so to speak, magical accomplishments, whose interdependence is both preemptory and unfathomable.

Because these adventures have had an overwhelming influence on the development of my affective life and of my imagination—I find proof just as much when I want it as when I do not—I will no doubt have to talk about them more explicitly later on. In the meantime, it is necessary only to remark how objectively moving and evocative the praying mantis is: it has as much right as the *Acherontia atropos* to be thought of as a *natural focus of overdeterminations*. Even its name *mantis* ("the prophetess") evokes higher preoccupations, and even if one did not know this meaning, the same resonances would still be brought out by the adjective *praying*. This is, however, most especially true of its habits: everyone knows that the female praying mantis devours her male during the very act of mating. I do not see how one could fail to be moved, at least unconsciously, by the terrible nuptial habits of such an insect. Now, the essential thing, as I see it, is that of all insects it is the one whose form most reminds one of a human form, mainly because of the resemblance of its rapacious legs to human arms. As for its ordinary pose, it is not that of someone praying, as common consensus would have us believe (one does not pray lying on one's stomach), but that of a man making love. This alone is enough to justify an obscure and constant identification. One can now see why men have always been so interested in the mantis and its habits, and why it is so aptly associated as much with love as with hatred, whose ambivalent unity it condenses so admirably. If one then thinks back to the convergent objective poossibilities of the popolar tree, one can understand in what way the image from *Ralentir Travaux* is likely to seem to many people indisputably, passionately, and tyranically exact, even if the reasons for this are not always evident.

In the light of these analyses, the following conclusions seem to suggest themselves:

First, the existence of concrete or abstract elements that are in and of themselves ideograms, that is to say representations that suggest, objectively and prior to each consciousness fleshing it out with personal adventures that relate to it, enough natural overdeterminations for these ideograms to be immediately and universally effective and moving. It is through their intermediary that one could explain the possibility of using an unknown person's lyrical associations for one's own ends. The problem of poetic communication would thereby be somewhat clarified; these ideograms form a common ground that properly belongs to no one and where everyone can feel truly at home, one can understand that it is possible, so to speak, to *recognize* and assimilate the syntheses of lyrical thinking, because the *personality* of the author as much as that of the reader is at these junctures at the mercy of their *impersonal* necessity. It will therefore be necessary to study carefully this resolution of the personal and the impersonal, the subjective and the objective, within and through these privileged elements.

The study of the syntheses of lyrical thinking, however, has also given rise to a second problem: that of the theoretical value one ought to give to such syntheses. There is no doubt that one often feels a certain enthusiasm when confronted by them. It would not be a matter of indifference if one could find out whether this is due to their being a sorry last resort, with nothing but the harmonic or musical consequences that constitute aesthetic pleasure, or whether they involve that joy that, according to Spinoza, indicates the passage from a weaker to a greater perfection. The preceding analyses have led us to surmise that it is rather a question of moving toward a more perfect *systematization of consciousness*. Thus one could be led to determine to what extent this need for sytematization is essential to human thought, and one could guide the latter toward supreme knowledge, that ancient consolation in which it never ceases, despite everything, to see its fate.

Only when this double question has been resolved—of the objectivization of ideograms and of the absolute value of systematizing thinking—will it be possible to truly determine the status one ought to give to lyrical activity and, more decisively, the scope and the interest of the satisfaction one should expect from this status.

V

THE OBJECTIVITY OF IDEOGRAMS

You can see the detour by which I was led, in the previous pages, to assume that certain objects and certain images, as a result of a particularly significant form or content, enjoyed a greater lyrical potential than others, this potential being valid for a very large number of individuals and sometimes for everyone, so that it seems to be an essential part of the element in question and consequently to have as much claim as this element to objectivity. The game of chess that I analyzed first of all from this perspective did not appear to be entirely lacking this capacity to be universally moving. The poplar tree revealed itself to be even more directly impressive, but it is above all, as we saw, the praying mantis that appeared, through its name, its habits, and its form, to be a magnificent example of this objectivity of ideograms.

THE PRAYING MANTIS

From biology to psychoanalysis

Certain objects and certain images, as a result of a particuarly significant form or content, enjoy a greater lyrical potential than others. This potential is valid for a very large number of individuals if not for everyone, so that it seems to be an essential part of the element in question and consequently to have as much claim as this element to objectivity.[1]

The praying mantis seemed to me, by its name, form, and habits, to present to a rare degree this objective capacity to act immediately upon one's affectivity, which is so useful in resolving the problem of the lyrical communication of the syntheses of the imagination. I therefore carried out some research to confirm my hypothesis on this matter and to understand, by taking a concrete example, how a representation could act upon each individual separately and, so to speak, secretly, in the absence of any symbolic character that would essentially derive meaning from its social use and the greater part of its emotional effectiveness from its role within the community.

I will record the results of my research without commentary, so as not to arouse any suspicion by seeming to demonstrate too much. These results also speak perfectly well for themselves.

Mantidae were probably the first insects to appear on the earth, given that the *Mantis protogea,* whose fossil print was found in the

---

[1] These pages, which make up the fifth chapter of a work to appear on the *mechanism of overdetermination in automatic and lyrical thinking and the development of affective themes in an individual consciousness* and is entitled *The Necessity of Mind and the Continuity of the Universe,* become truly meaningful only when read in the light of the ideas expressed therein. I have to make it clear, therefore, that I do not claim that the men who have carefully observed mantises have been impressed by their habits; I restrict myself to the affirmation that these insects and men being part of the same nature, I do not refrain from calling on

Oeningen Myocena, belongs to the Paleodictyoptera group as defined by Scudder, and whose traces are manifest from the Carboniferous Age on.

In his work *Die Antike Tierwelt* (Leipzig, 1909-1913), Otto Keller gives a reproduction of a Proserpinian coin from Metaponte on which a mantis is pictured next to an ear of corn, which, as we know, played such an important part in the mysteries of Eleusis. In the short commentary he gives on this insect (vol. 2, p. 460), the same author refers to the lexicographers and compilers Aristarchus and Suidus, who limit themselves to pointing out that the mantis lives in the reeds, and to Pseudodioskurides (πρι ἐνπορ. vol. 1, p. 158), who adds that the Indian mantis is, according to Keller's translation, "ähnlich und als Heilsmittel wirksam."[2]

This hardly helps us to understand why the Greeks gave it that name. Its name, μαντις, the prophetess, is found in French not only in *mantis* but also in a different written form in *rabdomancy, cartomancy, necromancy,* and so on. It is derived from μαινομαι, which means both "to be mad" and "to be inspired," and is connected to the Indo-European root *men*—which indicates the action of thinking. From this root are derived words corresponding to very diverse notions. It would not, however, be arbitrary to group these words together, if only because they share this appellation.

A. E. Brehm, in his book (which I leafed through in the French edition prepared by J. Künckel d'Herculaïs and published by Baillère), points out that Thomas Mouffet, an English naturalist of the sixteenth century, proposed three explanations for the attribution of the name

---

the former's behavior in order to account, if necessary, for the behavior of the latter in a given situation. For man is a special case only as far as he is concerned, and this study is really just an exercise in comparative biology.

[2] "Similar, and having medicinal properties." [Editor's note]

"mantis" to the insect in question. All three are equally untenable and are of no intrinsic interest, even as errors. It is probably the very same Thomas Mouffet who, in a passage quoted by J. H. Fabre (*Souvenirs entomologiques [Entomological Memories]*, vol. 5, ch. 20), recounts that the mantis, *when questioned by children who are lost, shows them the right way by extending its finger, only rarely, if ever, misleading them:* "Tam divina censetur bestiola ut puero interroganti de via, extento digito rectam monstret atque raro vel numquam fallat," a passage that is probably taken from his book entitled *Insectorum vel minimorum animalium theatrum* and is mentioned by other authors.[3] The same belief is also attested to in the Languedoc region (see Sébillot, *Le Folklore de la France [The Folklore of France]*, vol. 3, p. 323, n. 22).

This is not the only reason the insect is believed to have magical properties. A. de Chesnel recounts, in reference to Nieremberg, that Saint Francis Xavier was said to have made a mantis sing a canticle and tells of the case of a man whom this animal supposedly warned very opportunely to go back from where he came.

J. H. Fabre says he has often noticed that in Provence the mantis's nest is considered the ultimate remedy for chilblains and toothache, on the condition that it was gathered during a full moon. Sébillot (*Le Folklore* vol. 3, p. 330) notes that in the Mentone region the nest is said to cure sores. On the same subject, Eugène Rolland (*Faunes Populaires de la France [Popular Fauna of France]*, vol. 13, p. 117) refers to

---

[3] In fact, Eugène Rolland quotes it as such with reference to page 134 of the 1634 edition. His quotation has *altero pede* for *digito*, which seems more correct.

[4] Could one not think, in this case, that the fact that the grasshopper is considered by Italian peasants to be the prophetess par excellence (according to A. de Gubernatis [*Zoological Mythology*, London, 1872, vol. 1, ch. 7]) is the result of a very understandable confusion of this insect with the mantis?

Regius, *Mat. Médic.* (p. 32), but the poplar nomenclature he collected is particulary interesting: sometimes the mantis is called an "Italian girl" or a "phantom," and less explicably a "strawberry" or a "madeleine." More generally an ambivalent attitude emerges: On the one hand the insect is regarded as sacred, whence its usual name of *prégo-Diéou* ("pray-to-God"), with its variants and corresponding expressions in Parma, Portugal, the Tyrol, Germany, and Greece; on the other hand, it is considered diabolical, as testified by the symmetrical name of *prégo-Diablé* ("pray-to-the-Devil") that is found for example in the saying *brassiéjà coumo un prégo-Diablé* ("to gesticulate like a pray-to-the-Devil") (See *Revue de langnes romancs,* 1883, p. 295) and to which one should add the names "liar" and "bigot" given to it in Villeneuve-sur-Fère (a city in the Aisne region).

If we look now at the sayings used by children with respect to the mantis, we find two main themes: first, it is said to be a Prophetess[4] who knows everything, and especially the whereabouts of the wolf, and secondly, it is assumed that it is praying because its mother died or drowned. On this last point the testimony is unanimous.[5] In more general terms, it seems that we must agree with the opinion of De Bomare, who writes that in all of Provence, the mantis is regarded as sacred and that people avoid causing it the slightest harm.

This behavior is not exceptional: the facts recorded in the north of Melanesia are even more emphatic. Indeed, the natives of the Duke of

---

[5] I will quote the most explicit testimonies according to Rolland: *Prégo-Diéou, Bernado, Besto segnado, veni près de iéou, qué ta mayré es morto, Sus un ped de porto, qué toun payre est viéou sus un ped d'ouliéou* (Bernard the God-prayer, sacred beast, come here, for your mother is dead, on a doorstep, for your father is old, on a step of olive wood) (Arles); *Prégo Diéou, marioto, ta may qu'es morto, débat un peu dé porto; Te*

l'an réboundudo débat un ped de brugo (Pray to-God little Mary, your mother is dead, they buried her [for you] under a bush.) (Gascony); *Prego Diéou, bernado, qué tu mayré s'es négado* (Bernard the pray-to-God, your mother has drowned herself) (Aude); *Prégo, Bernado, qué Bernat es mort. Sus la porto del ort* (Bernard the prayer, Bernard is dead. At the garden gate) (Tarn).

York Islands are separated into two clans, one who recognizes as their totem Ko gila le, an insect that so closely resembles the leaf of a horse-chestnut tree as to be easily mistaken for one; and the other, the Pikalabas clan, who recognizes Kam, "which is doubtless the *Mantis religiosus*" (J. G. Frazer, *Totemism and Exogamy,* vol. 2, p. 120 ff.). Paul Eluard assured me that according to a work on ethnography whose title he unfortunately could not remember, in the New World certain indigenous populations of Mexico think of another mantid in the same way.

It is, however, the African data that are the most significant: for example, the happy mantis of the Cape of Good Hope is worshipped by the Hottentots (Khoi-Khoi) as a beneficent deity.[6] On this subject George Dumézil, professor of comparative mythography at the Ecole des Hautes Etudes, kindly pointed out to me a passage from Andrew Lang's *Myth, Ritual and Religion* (London: Longman's, 1887), in which the author analyzes the beliefs of the Hottentots and of the Bushmen.[7] According to these two tribes the supreme deity and creator of the world is precisely the mantis (Cagn), whose loves are, it seems, "pleasing," and it is especially attached to the moon, having made it out of one of its old shoes. Note that its main function seems to be to obtain food for those who beg for it, and that in addition it was devoured and vomited alive by Kwaï-Hemm, the devouring god (Bleek, p. 68). So the accent seems definitely to be on digestion, which is hardly surprising when one knows about the incredible voracity of the insect, which is a

---

[6] These Hottentots indulge at a certain time of the year in extremely lascivious dances, and the children fathered during this period are killed at birth (see E. S. Hartland, *Primitive Paternity,* London, 1910, vol. 2, p. 213). More generally, a better-researched study than this sketch would have to take into account the sexual mores of the small tribes who worship the mantis and the links that could connect them to the mythological use they make of this insect and its own habits.

prototype god. Among its other avatars, it is worthwhile to point out that when killed by thorns that once were men, and eaten by ants, it was resuscitated, its bones having been put back together again; in this adventure digestion still plays a certain part and links it to the very rich mythical cycle of the dispersed and resuscitated god of the Osiris type. The mantis worshipped by the Bushmen must furthermore be connected, as Lang remarks (*Myth, Ritual, and Religion,* p. 391, n. 1), to another mythical theme, that of the "separable force" (see Minos's lock of hair, Samson's hair, etc.). Indeed, it possesses a tooth in which all of its power resides, which it lends to those it sees fit.

It seems significant to me that in Provence, as in southern Africa, the mantis is specifically associated with teeth in a quite peculiar way. This association cannot simply be explained, in my opinion, by the connection between sexuality and nutrition that is found with the insect, even though this may seem decisive. It is now a well-known fact that teeth play an important part in sexual representations. A dream about teeth being pulled out is a reference either to masturbation or to castration or to giving birth, according to psychoanalysis, or to death, according to popular *Keys to Dreams.*[8] Moreover, in savage tribes where initiation rites at puberty do not involve circumcision, the extraction of a tooth often takes its place. All of these facts, then, show a remarkable coherence with each other and, as we will see later on, with the habits of the mantis.

So it seems that this insect has generally made an impression on

---

[7] Lang's main sources are, for the Hottentots, the writings of Peter Kolb in 1719 and of Thurnberg in 1792 and the study by Hahn, *Tsuni goam, the Supreme Being of the Khoi-Khoi;* for the Bushmen, the studies by Bleek, *A Brief Account of Bushman Folklore* (London, 1875) and by Orpen, "A Glimpse into the Mythology of the Maluti Bushman" (*Cape Monthly Magazine,* July 1874).

[8] See S. Freud, *The Interpretation of Dreams,* pp. 421-427 (trans. Strachey, New York: Avon Books, 1965), especially the long communication by Otto Rank quoted in a footnote and the examples of language and sayings that support this.

men.[9] This is doubtless due to an obscure identification that is facilitated by its remarkably anthropomorphic appearance.[10] We ought now to examine the reasons that are likely to have provoked it and that may have given it such a moving and lyrical content.

The family of Mantidae, according to the classification published in 1839 by Audinet-Serville, follows that of the Blattariae and precedes that of the Phasmidae or Specters.[11] It comprises fourteen species, the eleventh is that of the mantises properly speaking: these include the dessicated, superstitious, and herbaceous mantises; the brown-leaf mantis; the wide-appendix mantis (*Mantis latistylus*); the lobed, yellow-winged, and speckled mantises; the moon mantis; the simulacrum mantis; the patelliferrous, pustular, neighboring, and varied mantises; the mantis with two mamillae (*Mantis bipapilla*); the long-neck mantis; the cuticular, blemished, sullied (*inquinata*), and black-veined mantises; the hairy-feet mantis; the ornate, pious, praying, prasine, preaching, and vitreous mantises; the belted mantis; the phryganoid, ringed-feet, multi-striped, discolored mantises; the sister and pleasant mantises; the steel-blue mantis (*Mantis chalybea*); the red-

---

[9] Even the Chinese have been sensitive to it: in fact they raise mantises in bamboo cages and relish watching them fight (See Charles Darwin, *The Descent of Man and Selection in Relation to Sex* [New York: Modern Library, 1936]. Reference to Westwood's *Modern Classification of Insects,* vol. 1, p. 427).

[10] The anthropomorphic appearance of an element seems to me an infallible source of its hold on the human imagination. This is the case, for example, with vampires and mandrakes and the legends about them. It is by no means coincidental, in my opinion, that the belief in bloodsucking specters uses a bat as a kind of natural point of reference. The anthropomorphism of the bat runs particularly deep and goes well beyond the level of a general structural identity (the presence of true hands with a thumb opposed to the other fingers, pectoral breasts, a periodic menstrual flow, a free, hanging penis). As for the mandrake or mandragora (*Atropa mandragora*), The-

haunched mantis (*Mantis rubro-coxata*); the nebulous mantis; and, finally, the bright mantis and the Madagascan mantis.

This nomenclature is far from superfluous. The least one can say about it is that one comes across relatively few epithets using technical terms to recall the characteristic of its variety, and that one would not find a single one (apart from the last one) indicating the place where the insect is found in abundance or the name of the entomologist who discovered it, as is frequently the case with classification in the natural sciences. It must be said: These qualifications are in large part purely and simply lyrical.

The names of the genuses are usually even more precise: thus the twelfth one is the *epaphrodites* genus, literally "the ones who invite to love." As for the name of the first, *empousa,* this seems the most revealing to me. The word nowadays refers both to this variety of mantis and to a sort of fungus that lives as a parasite on certain insects, feeding off all their organs with the exception of the digestive tract. According to Littré, in the language of philosophers in the sixteenth century, it also referred to a fantastic imagination. In antiquity it was

---

ophrastus already calls it an *anthropo-morphon* and Columelle a *semi-homo.* Its remarkable poisonous, soporific, etc., qualities, and its property of being an effective antidote to snake poison finally assured its identification. See the interesting quotations in Gustave Le Rouge's *La Mandragore Magique (Téraphin, golem, androïdes, homoncules [The Magic Mandragoral]),* ed. H. Daragon, *1912.*

[11] *Histoire naturelle des insectes: Orthoptères* by Audinet-Serville (De Roret, 1839), pp. 133-214.

the name of a specter sent by Hecate and who, according to Hesychios of Alexandria, was capable of assuming several forms but had only one foot (whence its name).[12] The *Etymologicum Magnum* indicates that it is mentioned three times in Aristophanes (*The Frogs*, 1.293; *Ecclesiazusae*, 1.1056; and fragment 426), and, in addition, quotes a lexicographer according to whom the empousa was an infernal creature, having one foot made of bronze and the other made of donkey's excrement.[13]

I happened to be reading at the time *The Life of Appolonius of Tyana* by Flavius Philostratus, a book people believed would endanger the reputation that the Gospels had made for Jesus Christ, and in it I found, to my great surprise, a story relating to the adventures of an empousa and a young philosopher, a tale that brought together in singular fashion the habits of these specters and those of the insects that were to be referred to by the same name. It is a story of a young man who is seduced by a woman of extraordinary beauty whom he is about to marry, when Apollonius unmasks her by breaking her spell. Here are the two key passages:

> *This fine bride is one of the vampires, that is to say of*
> *those beings whom the many regard as lamias and*
> *hobgoblins. These beings fall in love, and they are devoted to*
> *the delights of Aphrodite, but especially to the flesh of human*

---

[12] Hecate appears for the first time in the Homeric hymn to Demeter composed for the mysteries of Eleusis, which is connected to the fact that on the coins from Metaponte reproduced in *Die Antike Tierwelt [The Ancient Animal Kingdom]* the mantis is associated with the ear of corn. It is worthwhile recalling, while on the subject, that Hecate rapidly became the goddess of sorcerers and necromancers and that she remained so throughout the Middle Ages, despite the efforts of the Church. See A. Maury, *La Magie et L'Astrologie dans les Antiquites et au Moyen Age, [Magic and Astrology in Antiquity and the Middle Ages]*, Didier et cie., 1862, p. 1884.

beings, and they decoy with such delights those whom they
mean to devour in their feasts.

And a few lines later:

And then she admitted that she was a vampire, and was
fattening Menippus up with pleasure before devouring his
body, for it was her habit to feed upon young and beautiful
bodies, because their blood is pure and strong. (The Life of
Apollonius of Tyana, *Book 4, 25, trans. F. C. Conybearne.*
London: Macmillan, 1912.)

One of Philostratus' translators, A. Chassang, points out that this
story aroused a good deal of attention and in particular was adapted by
Alexandre Dumas the Elder in chapters 22 to 24 of his *Isaac La-*
quedam. [14] But rather than comparing it with medieval conceptions of
incubi and succubi (although of intrinsic interest, these come from an
entirely different tradition and really—the quotations he gives only go
to prove this—have only a formal and, what is more, fairly loose
connection to the adventure of the empousa and the philosopher),
which would make one think more of vampirism, it seemed necessary
to read this story in the context of a double reality that makes vampirism seem tame by comparison: the habits of the mantises and human

[13] For more detailed information, consult
the article "Empousa" in Roscher's *Lexi-*
con and Pauly-Wissowa's *Realencyclop,*
and J. C. Lawson's work *Modern Greek*
Folklore and Ancient Greek Folklore,
Cambridge, 1910, pp. 174-175.

[14] Maury, *La Magie et l'Astrologie,* Introduction, p. XIV, n. 2.

anxiety about love that, seen in this light, appear to be less devoid of meaning than one would like to think.[15]

This feeling seems to me to correspond to a certain phase of affective development. It seems to me that it is particularly likely to become an exclusively passional theme. Thus Bychowski (*Ein Fall von oralem Verfolgungswahn [A Case of Oral Persecution Mania]*) analyzes the case of a victim who is convinced that he will be devoured by a prostitute before he has even approached her. I would be inclined more generally to link these fantasies with the development of most castration complexes that, as is well known, commonly originate in the terror of a toothed vagina, given that the assimilation of the entire body to the male member and likewise that of the mouth to the vagina are, so to speak, classics of psychoanalysis.[16] So it would not be impossible for the fear of castration to be a specific instance of the male's fear of being devoured by the female during or after copulation: a very precise repre-

---

[15] Ibid., "Eclaircissements historiques et critiques," pp. 447-450.

The story is also taken up by G. Flaubert in *The Temptation of Saint Anthony,* chapter 4, as I have just realized in rereading this work. Although I didn't notice it on my first reading, its content is significant enough to have overdetermined from the outset the ideogrammatic themes for which, in analyzing, I had to refer to the same work.

[16] There is a striking example of this in Mallarmé's sonnet "Une négresse par le démon secoué . . ." ("A negress shaken by the demon . . .," *Mallarmé,* trans. with an introduction by Anthony Hartley [London: Penguin, 1965], p. 16). This character is described as thrusting forward ". . . the palate of that strange mouth . . . pink and pale like a sea-shell." In the same text the use of *to taste, fruits,* and *glutton* as words with an erotic significance underlines the sense of confusion. Finally, the detail of her "laughing at the child with her naïve teeth" is all the more disturbing given that in the next line the child is called "the victim." There is no doubt that this sonnet lends itself to a study of overdetermination just as well as the texts I have analyzed previously; in any case, the remarkable coherence between the theme and the vocabulary should be pointed out.

sentation of this is provided objectively by the nuptial habits of the mantids, so great is the symmetry, or better still, the continuity, between nature and human consciousness.[17] This particularity adequately accounts for both the possibility and the effectiveness of objective ideograms, and it also corroborates the hypothesis already formulated of the systematic overdetermination of the universe.

In addition, one ought not to refrain in the present case from feeling an unequivocal attraction to the praying mantis. I will talk later on about my personal experiences, but there is no shortage of examples around me to illustrate this lyrical collusion: André Breton, for example, raised praying mantises in Castellane for two years in succession,[18] and Paul Eluard, whom I questioned on the presence in his home of a magnificent collection of mantises, admits to seeing the ideal sexual relationship in their love-making habits; the act of love, he says, diminishes the male and aggrandizes the female, so it is natural that she

---

[17] The insects also offer another particularity that could well be used as a direct representation of castration: the ability to resect a member voluntarily (autotomy). See Edmond Bordage's communication: *Comptes rendus de l'Académie des Sciences,* vol. 128, 1899, and *Bulletin Scientifique de France et de Belgique,* vol. 39, 1905.

[18] The same André Breton who writes in *Ralentir Travaux:*
> The women who in love hear the
>   wind pass through the poplar
>   trees
> The women who in hate are more
>   taut than praying mantises.

should use her ephemeral superiority to devour him, or at least to kill him. The case of Dali is even more applicable because of the impressive, comprehensive document on the relationship between love and homophagy that goes to make up his paranoiaco-critical study of Millet's *Angelus;* he was forced to bring in the fearsome insect that in fact unites these two savage desires.

Naturalists find in the praying mantis an extreme form of the close connection that often seems to combine sexual with nutritional voluptuousness, a connection that Dali has made immediately and intuitively explicit. On this subject one must at least cite, following Léon Binet, studies by Bristowe and Locket on the *Pisaura mirabilis cl.:* the female eats a fly offered by the male during coitus; those by Hancock and von Engelhardt on the *Oceantus niveus,* which has on its metathorax a gland whose contents are absorbed by the female immediately before mating, a peculiarity shared by a species of cockroach, the *Phyllodromia germanica;* those by Stitz on the scorpion-fly, which, during coitus, eats globules of saliva prepared for her by the male; the female of the *Cardeacephala myrmex* under the same circumstances feeds on food regurgitated by the male, who often offers it from his mouth to hers; and the female of the white-headed dectique, who opens the stomach of her companion, extracts the pocket of sperm from it, and devours it.[19]

It has been known for a long time that the mantis is not content

---

[19] W. S. Bristowe and G. H. Lockett, "The Courtship of British Lycosid Spiders and Its Probable Significance," *Proceedings of the Zoological Society,* London, 1926. In my opinion, this example is only convincing up to a point: one has no doubt to remember that the insect feeds during the very act of coitus. But the most important fact, that is, that the female draws this food from the body of the male either by devouring him or by absorbing the content of a special gland, cannot be stated categorically here.

See also B. B. Fulton, *The Tree-Crickets of New York: Life, History, and Bionomics,* 1915; O. W. Richards, "Sexual Selection and Other Problems of the Insects," *Biol. Reviews* 2, 1927; and William Morton's observation published in the *Journal of Heredity* 15, 1924.

The relationship between sexuality and nutrition, if not present in human be-with such half measures. Indeed, in 1784, J. L. M. Poiret in the *Journal de Physique* communicated the observation that he had made of a female mantis decapitating the male before mating with him and devouring him entirely after copulation. This story has been corroborated, with many aggravating details, by a recent and fine account by Raphaël Dubois. It was first thought, along with Paul Portier (see *Comptes rendus de la Société de Biologie,* vol. 82, 1919, with critical observations by Rabaud) that this cannibalism was explained by the fact that the mantis, needing albumin and protein to make its eggs, could find them nowhere in such great quantity as in its own species. Rabaud contested this hypothesis with several objections, noting in particular that the mantis does not eat the male when she needs this food. Thus, everyone prefers to rally to Raphaël Dubois' theory, which, it seems to me, does not exclude the previous one. This naturalist, noting that the decapitated cricket performs the reflex and spasmodic movements induced in it better and longer, and making references to the work of Goltz and H. Busquet—one had only to take away a frog's upper centers for it to immediately adopt the coital position that it normally only adopts in spring—wonders whether the mantis's goal in decapitating the male before mating is not to obtain, through the ablation of the inhibitory centers of the brain, a better and longer execution of the spasmodic movements of coitus. So that in the final analysis it would be for the female the pleasure principle that would dictate the murder of

---

havior, then at least is present in the human psyche, as certain perversions will attest. It would also be necessary to mention the embryonic differentiation of the functions of conservation and of reproduction, and of their organs, if the interpretation was not so subject to caution. It seems to me, moreover, that the psychoanalytic treatment of mental anorexia (when the subject refuses to feed him- or herself on various ethical or sentimen-

tal grounds), if it was attempted, and perhaps it has been, might well produce important results in this respect. Finally, it is an often-mentioned fact that women, after coitus, express and sometimes satisfy a craving to bite their lovers.

her lover, whose body, moreover, she begins to eat during the very act of making love.[20]

These habits are so well designed to disturb us that it seems that scientists have for once, to their credit, departed from their professional dryness. Thus Léon Binet, professor of physiology at the medical school in Paris, in his recent monograph entitled *La Vie de la Mante religieuse [The Life of the Praying Mantis]* is obviously troubled.[21] It is surprising enough at any rate to see him abandon for a moment his scientific detachment when he calls the mantis a "murderous lover" (p. 54) and allow himself a most disquieting literary quotation on the subject.[22] I would take this revealing weakness as a basis for interpreting the author's conclusion: "The insect seems to us very much like a machine with a perfect mechanism, capable of functioning automatically." Indeed, the assimilation of the mantis to an automaton—that is, in view of its anthropomorphism, to a female android—seems to me to be a consequence of the same affective theme: the conception of an artificial, mechanical, inanimate, and unconscious machine-woman incommensurable with man and other living creatures derives from a particular way of envisioning the relationship between love and death and, more precisely, from an ambivalent premonition of finding the one within the other, which is, in fact, something I have every reason to believe.[23]

---

[20] R. Dubois, *Sur les réflexes associés chez la mante religieuse.* Compte rendu de la Société de Biologie, 1929. See also the experiments performed by Daniel Auger and Alfred Fessard. One can see a photographic document representing this coitus-meal in J. H. Fabre, *Souvenirs entomologiques.*

[21] Vigot frères, 1931.

[22] This quotation is the following:
She exhausts, she kills, and it only makes her all the more beautiful.
A. de Musset, *The Cup and the Lip,* Act 4, Scene 1.

Nonetheless, I do not deny the existence of facts that alone could amply justify the conclusion in question. Such intersecting facts would, on the contrary, considerably increase the objective lyrical value of the praying mantis. Here, too, the reality exceeds our most ambitious hopes.

Indeed, besides the articulated rigidity of the mantis, which cannot fail to bring to mind that of an armature or of an automaton, the fact is that there are hardly any reactions that it is not also able to perform when decapitated, that is, in the absence of any central point of representation or of voluntary activity. In this condition it can walk, regain its balance, move one of its threatened limbs autonomously, assume the spectral position, mate, lay eggs, build an ootheca, and, quite astoundingly, fall down into a false corpse-like immobility when confronted by danger or following a peripheral stimulation.[24] I am deliberately using this indirect means of expressing myself because our language, it seems to me, has so much difficulty expressing, and our reason understanding, the fact that when dead, the mantis can simulate death.

Finally, one should not neglect the mimetism of mantises, which illustrates in a somewhat hallucinatory fashion the human desire for a return to an original insensibility that one must compare with the pantheistic conception of a fusion with nature, a frequent philosophical

---

[23] Not to mention the animal species, in which the male dies immediately after fecundating the female.

[24] There is a tendency to consider this behavior as purely automatic in every case. As E. L. Bouvier put it: "A phenomenon of differentiated sensibility, limited to a cataleptic tetanus and characterized by it" ("The Psychic Life of Insects," in *The Smithsonian Institute Annual Report,* 1918. Washington, 1920, pp. 451-459).

and literary translation of the return to a prenatal unconscious.[25] One has only to choose from the desert-colored *Eremiaphileus of Louxor;* the *Blepharis mendica,* which is flecked with white on a green background like the leaves of the *Thymelia mircophylla* where it lives; the *Theopompa heterochroa* of the Cameroon, which is indistinguishable from the bark of a tree; the *Empusa egena* of Algeria, which, not content with looking like a green anemone, stirs softly to simulate the action of the wind on a flower; the *Idolum diabolicum* of Mozambique, whose petal-shaped grasping legs are precisely tinged with crimson, white, and a greenish blue; the *Gongylus trachelophyllus* of India, which becomes "the picture of a brilliant flower that hangs in the air at times and that turns its most beautiful colors towards the brightest part of the sky"; the *Hymenopus bicornis,* finally, which one would have trouble distinguishing from a simple splendid orchid.[26]

The floral metamorphoses, in which the insect loses its individuality and returns to the vegetable world, are a culmination of both its astonishing capacity for automatism and the carefree attitude it seems to adopt to death. These properties are themselves a culmination of that which in its name mantis or empousa, that is, prophetess or specter-vampire; in its form, being of all the forms the one in which man can recognize his own; and in its pose of absent prayer or of the sexual act; and finally in its nuptial habits can have such a great effect on the intuitive sensibility of every individual.

It is now possible to account for the lyrical objectivity of certain concrete representations with a full knowledge of the facts, and to understand why they have the privilege of disturbing the affectivity of

---

[25] *The Temptation of Saint Anthony,* which has already been discussed in connection with the mantis, ends with a striking expression of this desire: seeing the three reigns of nature folding into each other ("then the plants become fused with the stones; rocks come to resemble brains, stalactites breasts, iron-

flowers tapestry adorned with figure," compare this with the mimetism of the mantises), the hermit cries out — these being his last words: "Oh, happiness, happiness! I have seen life being born" (This is also very significant from a psychoanalytic point of view in terms of the confirmation of identity: the return to the most diverse kinds of people and of arousing within them at the very least a common irrational curiosity.

It is not surprising that the great similarity between humanity's organic structure and biological development, combined with the identical external conditions of its physical world, should have considerable resonances in its psychic world, tending to produce within it a minimum number of similar reactions and consequently spawning within every mind the same affective tendencies and primordial passional conflicts, just as the identical mechanism of the senses brings with it—to a noticeably equivalent degree—identical a priori forms of perception and of representation. Nor does anything in these statements require the slightest explanatory hypothesis. On the contrary, the existence of elements in which others can recognize all or part of themselves no longer seems to be immediately inescapable. In other words, the possibility of a universe without objective ideograms appears on first sight to be conceivable; but on reflection, it does not take long to notice that it raises the same insurmountable problems in conceiving of a certainly determined world, yet one that is discontinuous and without any overdeterminations. Once again, the perfect isolation of a causal series is properly unthinkable. At the same time this lack of a causal series runs counter to experience, which never ceases to present multiple intersection and here and there provides overwhelming, undeniable testimony to their unfathomable interdependence: testimony, whose meaning is hidden and multivalent but infallibly hits its mark, and *the objective ideograms,* which are, in short, a *material realization in the external world of the virtual lyrical and passional elements of consciousness.*

---

the maternal womb) and concludes that he wants "to divide himself up everywhere . . . to penetrate every atom, to plumb the depths of matter—to be matter!" All the concrete associations of the last pages of the book would also lend themselves remarkably well to a search for lyrical overdeterminations.

[26] These examples are taken from A. Lefebvre, *Annales de la Société entomologique de France,* vol. 4; Léon Binet, *La Vie de la Mante religieuse;* Paul Vignon, *Introduction à la biologie expérimentale,* Paris, 1930.

VI

SYSTEMATIZATION AND DETERMINATION

It seems that all human striving for knowledge is reduced to a search for invariance in a fluctuating world.[1] I will confess that I for one am unable to remain satisfied with the common antinomy, perceiving no appreciable difference between the known and the unknown. I think that one would have to reflect only for a moment on this subject, provided one was free of theoretical prejudices, to understand how minimal the gap is that separates them. There is neither scepticism nor any excessive ambition here. I merely mean to say that knowledge and ignorance appear so equally imperfect and incomplete, so to speak, that the former makes do just as well with the most notorious inadequacies as does the latter with the most compromising actions, and that, this being the case, it is easy to see that words conceal two more or less equivalent aspects of the same situation. The opposition of difference and identity, of the mobile and the immobile, of the Other and the Same seems a more precise approximation. Science is quite accurately defined as the search for the unity of the cause behind the multiplicity of

---

[1] See C.-J. Keyser, *Mathematical Philosophy,* and E. Myerson, *Identité et Réalité.*

effects. That there is no discipline that has successfully managed to carry this project to completion in all areas, with the help of a principle that is apparently only related to one area, is a troubling fact, one that singularly exceeds the least circumspect expectations and that only appears to be able to explain itself by the hypothesis of a systematic overdetermination of all the elements. Indeed, it is as if the means of explaining each particular science was an *organization of plausibilities* made up from a given fact or a group of well-defined givens that were capable, because of the continuity of the universe, of producing a sort of indefinite concentric extension over all the other areas to the detri-

---

[2] διάκοσμον ἐοικότα *Parmenides,* frag. 8 (Diels, *Fragmente der Vorsokratiker,* 1905, vol. 1, p. 122), in the translation given by Ad. Diels in his introduction to Plato's *Parmenides,* Les Belles Lettres, 1923.

[3] A few examples will be useful here. I take them from the authors cited in the book by Matila C. Ghyka, *Esthétique des proportions dans la nature et dans l'art [The Aesthetics of Proportions in Nature and in Art],* whose own propositions I would be wary of putting forward. I suspect them of being too imbued with derisory mysticism or even more with an active aestheticism, and they bear witness in any case to a very vain inspiration. A number of them are nonetheless worth retaining.

It is a question of the proportion $\emptyset$ between two magnitudes a and b, such that $\frac{a}{b} = \frac{a+b}{a}$, that is to say, such that the greater one is to the smaller one as the sum of the two is to the greater one. It follows that the value of $\emptyset$ is given by the equation $\emptyset^2 - \emptyset - 1 = 0$, whose positive root is $\emptyset^1 = \frac{\sqrt{5}+1}{2} = 1,618$. Now $\emptyset^2 = \frac{2\sqrt{5}+5+1}{4} \frac{\sqrt{5}+1}{2}$, from which we

get, multiplying each time the two terms by $\emptyset$, $\emptyset^3 = \emptyset^2 + \emptyset$ $\emptyset^1\emptyset^3 + \emptyset^2 \ldots \emptyset^n = \emptyset^{n-1} + \emptyset^{n-2}$. That is, that in a geometric reason, reason $\emptyset$, when any one term is equal to the sum of the two previous ones, the series is both multiplicative and additive (See Marx Sarr in *The Curves of Life*).

In 1855, Zeysing was able, in his *Aesthetische Forschungen,* to apply these properties to the perfect accord between music and the porportions of the human body. Thus he discovered that a woman's body represents a series $\emptyset$ in which the magnitudes determined by the lines passing through the eyebrows, the base of the nose, the shoulders, the breasts, the navel, the tips of the fingers and the soles of the feet, are equal respectively to $\emptyset$, $\emptyset^2$, $\emptyset^3$, $\emptyset^4$, $\emptyset^5$, $\emptyset^6$, and $\emptyset^7$.

In 1835, Braun had already noticed that the arrangement of the grains of the sunflower was determined by two series of curves going in opposite directions to each other, with the proportion of the respective numbers being, according to the variety, 21/34, 34/55, 55/89, 89/144, or even 144/223. Here the numerator of each fraction is equal to the denominator of the previous one, and its denominator to the sum ment, of course, of the rigor of its understanding.[2] Indeed, the explanations of science intersect to such an extent that each science flatters itself with being able to account for the very existence of the others. Thus, one can currently see historical materialism and psychoanalysis, for example, reciprocally relating their constitution to the principle they have respectively adopted, each of these systems considering the other as a particular easily reducible given.

Even mathematics allows itself the most ambitious intrusions and finds the most precise proofs where one would least expect them, in botany and zoology, for example.[3] So it is generally permissible to

---

of the two terms of this previous one, such that the numbers that make it up are part of the series discoverd in 1202 by Fibonacci, a series that not only has properties analogous to those of the $\emptyset$ series, but in which the relationship between the two consecutive terms also tends toward $\emptyset$, as pointed out by Kepler (in his book *De nive sexangula*), who had also seen its function in the growth of plants, something corroborated by Schooling in 1912.

In 1875 Wiesner, a student of phyllotaxis, pointed out that the optimum angle of the spiral arrangment of leaves around the stem is $\alpha = 137°30'27''95''' = \frac{360°}{\emptyset^2}$.

The following year, in 1876, Fechner and the psychophysicians, giving their subjects a series of rectangles to choose from that were constructed according to varying proportions, found an almost unanimous preference for the one whose dimensions conformed to the $\emptyset$ relationship, a relationship that governs, moreover, the proportions of postcards, official quarto-sized paper, bars of chocolate, the pyramid of Cheops, the five platonic polyhedra, and the molecular chemistry of the *Timeus*.

One ought to mention, finally, the studies by Arcy Thompson (*Growth and Forms*)

and by S. Coleman (*Proportional Form*), which conclude by showing that the shell of the *Heliotis splendens* in particular is a logarithmic spiral (Bernoulli's *spira mirabilis*), that is, a spiral whose radius increases geometrically when the angle increases arithmetically, and is consequently constructed on the basis of the "sublime triangle," an isoceles triangle whose side and base conform to the $\emptyset$ relationship, a relationship that also determines the proportions of the star-shaped pentagon that makes up the armature of marine and flower organisms.

These facts are not intended to be used for the benefit of aesthetics. This would be to privilege abstract, formal considerations over the immediately emotive semantic richness of the lyrical content, thereby arbitrarily depreciating all its psychic and passional importance for some particularly uninteresting harmony. It is nonetheless necessary to indicate a mathematical overdetermination of the universe where there is one, even if it considers as ingenuous the famous proposition of a mathematician to enclose the world in an equation containing only a few unknowns.

affirm that experimental data can be decoded using several keys and systematized from several points of view, whose number is not a priori determinable, and each constitutes a particular method of knowledge, which because of this fact itself appears as a sort of systematization. One is thus led to formulate the problem of the value of the lyrical imagination in the same terms and to examine whether it can be of as much service in the area of affective representations and passional themes as are, for example, geometry and dialectics, whose triple quality of being genetic, absorbent, and systematizing is clear elsewhere. *In short, it is simply a question of translating the fact that understanding is always more or less reduced to integration;* from this point of view, the perfect science would be nothing more than the effective awareness of the multiple coherence of the elements of the universe, an apperception that would quite likely bring about not only significant changes in the way we see and feel (it does not seem arbitrary here to play on the double meaning of certain words, both abstract and concrete) but also the adoption of a truly moral, even metaphysical position. That is the content I would like to give to the idea of salvation, which should not be considered excessively honorable, but that nonetheless deserves better than the pitifully low esteem in which we are more or less forced to hold it today because of its ideological inconsistency, if we stretch indulgence to the point of not judging a book by its cover.

Whatever the case may be, and to return to the thick of the debate, I would be happy if one were to agree with me that in the pages above I have placed the problem of the value of lyrical thinking in the necessary perspective and on the most solid ground. I do not have the least illusion about the answer I propose. I have been in a better position than anyone to see how limited my research has been, how indecisive its results, how vague its approximations. Nevertheless, I think that I have the evidence on my side when I affirm that if lyrical thinking does not have the interest in systematization I expect it to have, it has none at all —none that is valid, of course.

With dreams, the work is more than half complete. Indeed, if one agrees to consider the mechanisms that psychoanalytic research has, if not discovered, then at least defined (condensation, overdetermination, transfer, etc.) as *processes of the affective systematization of representations* that, owing to the necessities of action, had at first seemed disparate—and it appears difficult to assign them any other role—it is clear that oneiric signs, even though there are dreams and then there are dreams, are the least negligible of signs, and what is more, that they constitute particularly reliable documents, elaborated as they are according to relatively autonomous processes.

The same cannot be said for lyrical thinking, which is accomplished through means that are far from being above all suspicion, and about which there is no reason to believe that it is provoked by an urgent need rather than by laziness or forfeiture. It must be noted, however, that the example of dreams, a phenomenon whose elementary and independent nature I was keen to recall earlier, shows that the necessity of the mind is capable of identifying or of associating by itself the appropriate representations, such that one is led to wonder *whether the function of lyrical thinking in waking life is not to figure in a similar manner the elements it needs when the requirement makes itself felt,* that is, when several representations have already overdetermined its content; the content is able for this reason to best fill the ideogrammatic role of systematization that preexisted it and to which, in the last analysis, it owes its appearance. So it is that several irregular rocks put together carelessly leave a certain gap between them, the shape precisely defined, such that the shape of the rock that would fill this interstice is strictly determined in advance, the determinism of this space being as rigorous as any other. Similarly, it seems that an accumulation of convergent representations predetermines all or part of the conditions that the representations they need to present a flawless coherence will have to meet. It follows that this representation exists virtually because of the existence of the previous ones, and at the first contingent prompting, passing from potential to actual, it will impose itself on one's consciousness.

Those are at any rate the thoughts that occurred to me during the analysis of a recent example of undirected associations. While waiting for my train, my eyes chanced upon a metal plaque, indicating perhaps some junction, with a white *M* painted on it. I then remembered that this letter happens curiously enough to be the initial of the first name of the only three women with whom my relationships have taken on an exceptionally serious character, and of the nickname I had given to one of them; then I thought of the test of the upside-down *M* in the hand (an expression that seemed to my very idle attention to provide in and of itself sufficient evidence). I thought of a wound shaped like an *M* on which vinegar was poured, as a torture or an initiation rite, while I had a fairly clear visual image of a hand opening and revealing an *M* on its palm, an *M* that, because of the way its points were turned toward the fingers, looked like a *W.* Without dwelling on the strangeness of the vision, I allowed my thoughts to wander and noted that *W* and *M* were the initials of a woman to whom that very morning I had just sent a book, and that these two intertwined letters formed the monogram that figures on the chairs in my parents' dining room, a cabalistic-looking sign that made a strong impression on me during my childhood, and whose meaning I asked ten times over, never content with the very reasonable answer given to me, which had to do with the initials of the people from whom the furniture had been bought. It seemed to me, however that I noticed the monogram more recently, and indeed it did not take me long to remember (but this investigation put an end to the association) that the day before I had seen an almost identical design presented as a condensed written form of the sacred monosyllable AUM in René Guenon's book *Le Roi du Monde [King of the World],* the pattern of which I had wanted to compare with that of the book I was about to send to this woman I mentioned above, and whose initials were precisely *W* and *M.*

I like the fact that there is nothing here that lies outside the bounds of the most banal experience: it becomes all the more important, then, to account for the unexpected representation that appeared so punctually to draw together the other elements, and in which I have been able to find no precise substratum, despite searching deep into my memory. It could always of course be a memory of an unidentified dream or of some disfigured hypermnesic image *whose disfiguration, moreover, could not fail to be significant.*[4] It seems far more economical to assume that there was a kind of ideogrammatic crystallization (and in this instance, of a somewhat hallucinatory nature) whose function was to associate the many intersections that surfaced right away, and that by their very existence determined and implied the content, assigning it the necessary and sufficient property of explaining, as much by perception as by reflection, the fact that an upside-down *M* is a *W*, and of presenting the two signs as simultaneously joined together. As for the word *crystallization,* it was by no means chosen at random: indeed, how could one fail to notice that the unusual placement of their images between virtuality and reality, their latent existence *in solution,* so to speak, is analogous to those highly unstable states studied and known in chemistry as *phenomena of supersaturation* in which, upon a minimal but well-defined excitation, a precipitate of the invisible dissolved substance condenses and appears as if it were produced from thin air. But instead of extending the comparison to include circumstances of production (between the rise in temperature and slow cooling down on the one hand, and the passions building up and being calmed down on the other) in which the curve is obviously identical, it is doubtless wiser to draw attention to the ease with which such analogies become specious when one asks more of them than the modest and empirical service of reciprocal clarification that they can provide.

In short, I will be quite satisfied even if the above analysis has cast but a little light on the way in which lyrical thinking can perform its

---

[4] I am alluding to the fact that a few days later, and in connection with something quite different, I remembered that as a child I had read in an illustrated newspaper the story of a certain Ismail the Bulgarian who used a dagger to sculpt a cross into the hands of his prisoners. It is possible that the image of the hand was provided by an unconscious reminiscence of this torture, even though the way the fingers themselves form an *M,* and the fact that this letter is at the same time the initial of the word *hand* (*main*), are sufficient to overdetermine its appearance.

systematizing function, so that the value of the syntheses one has seen it achieve could at least be measured approximately. What one has is an irreducible effort toward that perfect affective lucidity whose consequences, however unpredictable they might be, could only be very far-reaching and could not be discredited without at the same time discrediting oneself. What is called poetic activity, based as it is on the overdetermination of the universe, had seemed viable; as itself an overdetermination, and one of the most effective ones in this area, it now seems neither replaceable nor—insofar as it is carried out as it should be, that is to say in a methodical and not an aesthetic manner—devoid of validity.[5] As a result the benefit gained from such a succession of lyrical associations is measured by the increase in immediate sensibility following its assimilation and is also a function of the number and intensity of representative focal points that it condenses and overdetermines in a personal myth. These focal points are indefinitely contagious because of their epidemic development, so one can easily imagine that these two registers coincide in all individuals who are sufficiently motivated to *inhabit* the syntheses that they make their own. In this light, the expression "the beauty of a poem" has hardly any discernible meaning. On the contrary, the lyrical power or objectivity of a given representation or association will be correctly understood in terms of the force, stability, and generality of its uses, and particularly, as concerns each person, in terms of the greater or lesser degree of necessity of its integration into one's personal affective development.

Indeed, at a deeper level it is this affective development that is at stake, and one might undertake a decisive study along these lines. I

---

[5] These considerations characterize quite well my position within surrealism. Anxious to situate them precisely with respect to the ideas, for example, expressed in the *Manifestoes of Surrealism* (trans. Richard Seaver and Helen R. Lane, Ann Arbor: University of Michigan Press, 1969), I would be willing to align them with the following passage: "By slow degrees the mind becomes convinced of the supreme reality of these images. At first limiting itself to submitting to them, it soon realizes that they flatter its reason, and increase its knowledge accordingly" (p. 37), or even with this definition: "Surrealism is based on the belief in the superior reality of cer-

have said many times already what serious consequences I for one expected from it, consequences that would almost certainly be located beyond the two terms of the central problem of the necessity and the freedom of the mind.

It is a question of systematization, of knowledge, of knowledge of necessity. Is it then a question of freedom, as a certain well-known proposition would have it—a proposition that could, it seems, figure among the most blatant of accredited errors? We would not dare to claim as much. Consciousness is as lucid with respect to the determiner as to the determined, to which in its ignorance it was relegated. It is thus only a question of understanding the determination oneself, of identifying with the determination itself.

I thus intend to give some indication of how this concerns me more personally.

---

tain forms of previously neglected associations, in the omnipotence of dreams, in the disinterested play of thought" (p. 26). I, of course, leave the responsibility for the expressions "superior reality" and "disinterested play of thought," which seem to me to be either inexact or hypothetical, to André Breton.

VII

THE DEVELOPMENT OF
IDEOGRAMMATIC THEMES

*Reality appears in its development as
necessity itself.*

Hegel

I alluded in the previous pages to the circumstances in which I saw
and captured a praying mantis for the first time. I pointed out in this
connection that these circumstances seemed to me more and more to
form a disconcertingly coherent whole. This could not be more exact.
But I must add that I am at the same time more and more certain that
there is nothing out of the ordinary about these trivial details, and
nothing uncommon about the distraught manner in which I lived them
when I was that age. So when I feel the memory of them grow inside
me against my will and take on legendary proportions, I am alarmed
above all by the imminent personal defeat this metamorphosis cannot
but prefigure, a metamorphosis that I am severe enough to consider as
merely a late and tendentious exultation, delusively nurtured by some
premature yet irremissible nostalgia.

This is of little importance: I will take this short space of time as
my point of departure all the same, because in view of the perfect
coherence that has finally come to light within the memories that I
retain of this time, however much I exploit the ultimate resource of
seeing in it less an accidental and meaningful mask than the very
principle of these memories' exclusive subsistence, the problem is still

not resolved and is at best more clearly articulated. Indeed, it remains inexplicable that the many elective affinities that seem to have presided over the organization of the details obsessing me should have been acquired independently and, to express myself a little more mysteriously than usual, as if by virtue of the *force of things,* which is such an eminently prophetic characteristic that it is hardly possible anymore for me to measure them by ordinary standards. I, of course, force myself to think of this apparent state of affairs as merely retrospective, but I cannot without excessive complacency ignore the fact that very ordinary events that actually took place lend themselves unreservedly to being interpreted as an exact prefiguration of my entire affective development. These may be just symptoms, admittedly; but I now realize that there is nothing in my life that has not been strictly faithful to them. I hardly regret having been so dependent, not knowing whether this obedience (blind and passive if anything ever was, and for a very good reason) is due to a great insufficiency or to a great morality. I cannot decide, for I obviously have too many bad motivations not to mistrust the good reasons that I would invoke in this regard. I will continue to let things run their own course, but perhaps with greater lucidity, my resolve strengthened by this original unity, which I have discovered through analysis, within the multiplicity of emotive themes.

So it was one summertime in Royan: I had captured with great excitement this awesome green mantis that I had so much wanted to possess. I can say nothing about this capture except that it was followed very shortly by that of another insect no less evocative of death than the praying mantis: the *Acherontia atropos,* about which at the time I knew nothing of what either Poe or Strindberg had said of it, and that I had never even seen before catching it in the early hours on Cypress Street (so named no doubt because people did not want to call it Cemetery Street, as it would have been natural to do, for that is what it was). It squealed when I took it between my fingers, just as a bat would have squealed. I was terrified: it was so incredible that a moth should squeal, and this particular one had so much significance for me. Indeed, for a long time I had been afraid of seeing a hard, white death's head with holes in it glowing at night behind the black windowpane of my bedroom. Then I began to have doubts about the possibility of such a fantastic apparition, but I feared that someone, getting it into his head to make up for nonexistent ghosts, would have the idea of cutting a death's head out of glazed paper and sticking it on my window. It seemed to me that the vision I would have had of it would have been no less *true,* so convinced was I that the nasty practical joker would only have been an unconscious and innocent instrument that the invisible powers that wanted to terrify me would have used. I had in fact only increased my anxiety by making its object more likely. Yet in taking hold of a death's-head moth, I had the feeling that I would forevermore be in control of the sentiment I dreaded. When I got home, instead of putting the butterfly away with the others in one of the boxes of my collection, I pinned it to the wall, with its lugubrious insignia in full view: there is no doubt that this act should be seen as a magical apotropaic rite.

I now come to the third adventure: it was in the evening at the seaside. I knew as little as anyone could about love and about the commerce that certain people are reduced to making of it. As was my wont, I was sad. I will refrain from describing the painful emotions of those ill-informed adolescences that, for want of knowing their actual outcome, can never properly locate their despair or their joy. There is in effect no way of accounting for them, aside from the very crude falsification of literary psychology, which I would tolerate even less here than elsewhere. In any case, everyone can refer to individual memories. So I was leaning with my elbows on the parapet to the beach, away from the compact throng of passers-by. A woman dressed in a green coat, as green as the praying mantis I had just captured, came up to me. I had until that moment never known any woman personally; I withdrew instinctively. She asked why I was alone and sad; I ought to come with her. "Why?" "You'll see: you'll have a good time." I refused; she was peeved at my refusal and disappeared into the crowd, where I was to glimpse her and catch her eye a few moments later. This woman's voice was so soft, its tone so distant, her inflections so persuasive, and her words of such a rare, precise slowness and correctness, that these qualities, although all to her credit, considerably worsened the state of real fear that she had aroused in coming up to me. By refusing her incomprehensible invitation I had, and still have, the feeling of having committed a decisive injustice. But I yielded to an anxiety that was stronger than me, which I cannot justify by some problematic threat from my family, and that appears to me to be due to a latent dread of love, nurtured all through a solitary and extraordinarily ill-adapted childhood.

However I look at it, this encounter, which I soon understood a little better, is the only event in my life that has left me with anything resembling remorse. I know what cynical explanation one should probably give to it. It is the one I decided upon. Nevertheless, it seems to me to be unable to fully account for this woman's attitude or for mine, and one cannot deny, all things considered, that the adventure had all the appearances of distinction, and I insist that neither she nor I lacked such distinction, to the point where my present willful deprecation could look like a very disagreeable cautiousness.

Here are the facts; I have not embroidered upon them, but, on the contrary, there are just a few simple connections between them; the butterfly is associated with death, the woman with love, the mantis with both love and death. I had never noticed until then this coherence, which is so elementary and obvious, and also without any objective consequences.[1] For me it was just a question of a group of memories, each in and of itself very moving and that were only linked together, it seemed to me, in order to refer to almost simultaneous events. I will try now to systematize the progressive diversification and transformation of the ideogrammatic themes of my adolescence. As we will see, it will have been neither pointless nor arbitrary to introduce them through the story of the affective traumas that beset me in this memorable month of

---

[1] This does not mean that the association of concepts illustrated by these elements has not always preoccupied me. See infra., "Supporting and Supplementary Documents," VI, p. 138.

the summer of 1928, when I saw opening before me the Atlantidian gates of orichalc of the world of passions.

Again, I will be wary of any psychological description. Indeed, nothing—I will never tire of repeating—can appear more dangerous or more arrogant to anyone who normally demands some degree of rigor and precision. So I will restrict myself to communicating these rare documents as testimony that I can bring forward, even if it means linking them together with remarks of a quite clinical dryness.

As I have already mentioned, I was at the time extraordinarily ignorant of the most elementary facts about sexuality, which were to be revealed to me in increasingly explicit dreams. Along with this I also harbored the gravest pessimism with respect to the world and to myself, and a whole gloomy metaphysics developed out of it, which was vague, unstable, and wearying. So almost everything about this anxiety was indistinct, and it was then that I became acquainted with a woman who, under these circumstances, was to attract me more than any other. Her witch-like ways, her maliciousness, which was at once incomparable and disinterested, could not but seduce me. A downright mythomaniac, she was able in some way or other to act out imaginary roles from important events presented on the front pages of the newspapers every day. I hated her as much as I desired her. On the very night she became my mistress I tried to strangle her. At the same time, she had me read works popularizing so-called esoteric doctrines from which they only retained the colorful features; although I had information from better sources, I was still curious about their content because they came to me from a woman who, to take her at her word, had killed one of her lovers with a magic mirror and from whom it seemed to me I could expect the most fearful secrets. It is typical that the texts I was able to write at the time do not yet make a clear distinction between meta-physical and erotic fantasies, which cannot simply be attributed to the somewhat dubious romanticism with which they were tainted to some degree.

Yet little by little the confused possibilities became more clearly defined through being concretely enhanced every day by emotions and unusual readings. In this way two themes were formed that were each capable in turn of producing disturbing representations: the theme of the femme fatale and the psychasthenic theme whose persistent influence I noted in the texts analyzed earlier. The reason for this is that for a long time they had an exclusive monopoly on the active forces of my sensibility and my imagination, reigning supreme and unchallenged over them.

First of all, it is not difficult to see how the concept of a femme fatale of a different nature from man, and in any event dangerous and mortal, could have originated in the kind of confused and passive emotional state that has no doubt been brought out by the facts recounted earlier. It is also not difficult to understand that it could not be immediately free from all metaphysical attributes. So it was that in my daydreams I unfailingly associated it with two texts, and it is not a matter of indifference that they both were parts of "sacred" works that, appropriately enough in view of the results that my analysis of the concept of dynasty brought to light, dated back to classical antiquity.

The first is an evocation from the Song of Songs (6:10): "Who is this arising like the dawn, fair as the moon, resplendent as the sun, terrible as an army with banner?" an evocation that, I had not noticed prior to reading it, was cited in a Scandinavian novel in which the central motivation was vengeance and whose cover I liked to look at, for it bore the publisher's insignia: the unfinished, threatening Tower of Babel illuminated through the clouds by the oblique rays of the setting sun, which seemed to illuminate nothing but the enormous and always deserted openwork spiral of this dazzling and imposing edifice that Lautréamont was to continue in a worthy manner later on in the *Chants de Maldoror.*[2]

---

[2] I have since ascertained that the Tower of Babel was built in order to be seen at dusk. This was originally its sole purpose. On this question it would be indispensable to consult J. G. Frazer's *Le Folklore dans L'Ancien Testament* [*Folklore in the Old Testament*], Part 1, Chapter 5, trans. Audra Geuthner, 1924, pp. 125-133.

The second text, taken from the Shvetashvatara Upanishad (1: 4-5), despite being clearly metaphysical, seemed for that very reason all the more compatible with the concept of the femme fatale:

> *Consider That Thing now as a wheel with a hub,*
> *thrice encircled, with sixteen rims and fifty spokes, twenty*
> *knots and six groups of eight, made of all things, tied*
> *together with a rope, turning in three directions of which*
> *the sole illusion was born from two causes: like a river*
> *with five currents, issuing from five fountains, with per-*
> *ilous undercurrents, whose original source is the quintuple*
> *knowledge, like the five backwashes of which the tidal bore*
> *is the quintuple sufferance with fifty arms on five levels.*

It was on the aforementioned theme of interminable reveries. I used the name and the concrete appearance of Antinea for the wonderful, mortal creature that my imagination never tired of reinventing, and whom I worked into a mythology created specially for this purpose. The result was a series of complex descriptions in which ideas and images became entangled in a rather unpleasant mixture.[3] During this time my metaphysical concerns, contaminated by this dissolute imagination that only encouraged complete apathy, culminated in a real, intellectual disintegration, whose characteristics it did not take me long to compare to those of the psychasthenia I found described in Pierre Janet's book *Les Névroses* [*Neuroses*], a work I had just gotten to know. It soon became a matter for me of an immense enterprise of experimentation and of destruction. I exhausted myself observing the passage

---

[3]Here is one example:
> *The frippery that adorns is the*
> *test of her body's splendor; on the*
> *night's tears, she bore witness that*
> *poetic creation overflows time and*
> *superficial metamorphoses. She*
> *made herself a path of light which*
> *unveils to her the statues she*
> *passes, and this is why each min-*
> *ute is for her a crucifixion, and*
> *death a throw of the dice. Madness*
> *has made its way into her mind,*

from being awake to being asleep, and thus for long hours, while I tried in vain to *fall asleep consciously* without seeing that I might as well have gone in search of darkness carrying a lamp, I was the locus of the most astonishing tactile hallucinations. I had such a singular sensation of gravity that I could only remain aware of my recumbent body with what was in truth an imperceptible effort. My gestures wandered off brusquely into strange deserts. These kinds of ground swells attacked me insidiously and rendered me in a sense *formless*. What I wanted more than anything was to break the interdependence of my body and my thought. I wanted to cross the border of my skin, live on the other side of my senses; I practiced watching myself from a given point in space.

One Sunday I went to the asylum at Saint-Anne to attend a class on pathological psychology: a woman who was supposedly mad was introduced, and she expressed herself as follows: "I am not living, but someone is living me, when I sleep, someone sleeps me: it is as if I were dead and I were watching over myself." I enthusiastically adopted

---

but she knows its raison d'être and its games and its signs, and sometimes flatters it like a great, pensive animal, the sole confidant of a mortal secret: then she stands up straight and disdainfully attends a slow funeral which she knows is false. Her eyes lurk in that which cannot be transferred, and one understands that they are the flowers in which dread is multiplied before being resolved, and why they guard their looks so jealously, as if they carried the secret of a mysterious epithalamium.

The contour of the clouds and shimmer of the running water show her to those who are informed of the goal of their journey and who have not interpreted

the general language on the other side of the stars. Her form becomes clearer in the shimmer of the running water, as does the geometry of her incomprehensible jewels; and those who have left the day's dispersions where the men are isolated like small islands solely in order for sleep and the regions of absence to be withdrawn, those whose heredity does not stop with man, who are inscribed at each step on the final list, who see the log steel rail show through which crosses her blue eyes like an opal at the bottom of the river, long forgotten, whereas all of the faith in the world, once lost, has accumulated in her.

this language, unrivaled in its precision, and I deliberately became involved in the culture of psychasthenia, understanding this word to mean the disturbances of the perception of personality, particularly insofar as it occupies a determined position in space. It was not a matter for me of the a priori form of sensibility, but of perceptible space and even, to be more precise, of what is expressed when one says not space, but *a space:* a disturbing expression that defines something that is at the same time empty and well circumscribed.

At times the impression of growing smaller plunged me into despair or humiliation, and at other times I would abandon myself unreservedly to the unconsciousness of a continuous lethargy containing dream scenes every now and then, in which it seemed to me I was as uncompromised as possible.[4] While awake I let myself go even more than when I was asleep. When I was affected by outside pressures that sometimes forced me to act less mechanically than usual, I went through short periods of excitation, but in those circumstances in which I had to make contact again with the things to which I was least well-

---

[4] Whence the following text:

Self-resorption; for a long time my body was too big for me, but now I have been driven back into a tiny little space and I am not always sure I can stand up in it. Concern that I am going to get even smaller. It seems to me, however, that I have reached the limit, and it is not really possible for me to be completely annihilated in the end. I wander about in my body as if I were in a large empty cage. I do not fill out my body; I have been driven away from it, I have retreated little by little and here I am now, minuscule and unhappy, just like a little bell. But my life ought to just continue along its necessary path. It is too weak now, too far driven from its unhappy body, too small; it goes along from death to death as it gets smaller and smaller.

105

adjusted, I was prey to a sentimental pessimism that really had nothing to do with the phenomenon itself, which had primarily to do with the senses. In the meantime I would write truly delirious texts that I felt compelled to act out, while life, without being cheerful, gave an as-yet distant reason for putting up with it. I gave in to the demon of interpretation, and when I emerged from my exhausting experiments I summed up what my hypnagogic sensibility had brought me as follows:

> *I have been taken away from my body. It's like a piece of paper that you tear off when you want to unglue it. Each particle of my flesh was being ripped off. Each time it seemed to me as if I was being poured into a funnel. Now my body is alive but I am dead, being no longer in my body, someone having taken my place. While I am asleep I become a piece of material, a kind of sponge; I say this because I am all perforated and icy liquids penetrate me through and through.*
>
> *There was a space between me and my skin, and it was getting bigger. I was becoming space, black space where nothing can be put. I saw clearly that my body was no longer real. My lucidity became frightening: in my body everything was crumbling and melting. I naturally saw this as a swirl of barely distinguishable molecules and dusts, since I had real eyes and everything comes down to that: swirling dusts; things have no end and are not separated out. Everywhere there is nothing but swirling dust. And I felt myself beginning to resemble, not to resemble anything, but just to resemble. Millions of infinitesimal particles whirled about and swirled together and I was connected to all of them as if on axes that turn above circular voids. I felt the pressure of the strings. I was being turned faster and faster. Hands took me by the shoulders, closed through my body, and went away. I invented spaces that took convulsive possession of me. I was especially afraid of those*

that were round and liquid-like. I made unheard-of efforts
to free myself from this world of dusts driven wild by the
wind. Other people believe in their cars, their houses, their
will, their ideas, but science proves what is confirmed by
experience: there is nothing but gray dusts in the place of
man. What is more, I saw this, and in the infinity of gray
dust, I could no longer tell where my place was.

These tortures, which did nothing for me and that I reached only after hours of enervation while I lay in wait for sleep, not aware of the role of provocation, finally wore me out. Yet I still retained some fondness for a general theory of psychasthenic realization, which I had sketched out at the time and at the end of which the kind of depersonalization through assimilation to space that emerges from the lines quoted above, was considered the supreme metaphysical process.

So in both cases, as much in these attempts at an experimental metamorphosis as in the daydreams in which I imagined myself at the mercy of a superhuman creature, the same feeling of self-annihilation seems to predominate. It seems worthwhile to have provided a few texts that have the advantage, however clumsy they are, of being truthful documents on the lyrical unity of an affective development that was ultimately to find its most moving and condensed representation in the vision of the feminine automatons: figures of splendid sterility, of mechanical perfection with no human flaws, of death as much as of love, of those artificial femmes fatales as absolute as mantises in their lust and their murder, and which mad inventors build by the light of giant electrical sparks.

The schematic character of this concise overview doubtless deprives it of all its persuasive power; but it was nonetheless important to show through a number of examples how the analyses that are the object of this work allow one to see the ways in which one could envisage the development of the affective life. I wanted simply to indicate one possibility. Each day brings concrete elements to the conscious mind that it does not integrate as indifferently as it seems and whose mutual isolation is only an effect of ignorance. It is perhaps not so difficult to discover their infinite coherence and to become increasingly aware of the organization that is immanent to them and of the central passional themes, which have always determined this coherence.

This is the work proper of what I would gladly call *lyrical lucidity,* to which I attached, as was seen, very great hopes. What is more, how, in a world of overdetermination, could the necessity of mind not have the last word?

CONCLUSION

If one is not oneself used to giving overdeterminations the attention they deserve, one might be tempted to consider their systematic presence as an exeptional circumstance. Viewed in this light, the above analyses will unquestionably seem to be typical of an appropriate insanity. As for the general hypotheses that provide a commentary upon them, they will in all likelihood be considered as lacking any objective foundation and any theoretical value. It seems worthwhile anticipating such an objection by pointing out that overdeterminations, like coincidences, are not only normal, but unavoidable.

Let us recall the following well-known problem: are there two people in London who have exactly the same number of hairs? The answer is that one can mathematically assert that there are not only two people, but several thousands of times two people, who have an identical number of hairs, the very simple reason for this being that the number of inhabitants in London is far greater than the number of hairs on a particularly dense head of hair.[1] No one, however, would not at first think that such a conjunction was miraculous. Not only is it a fact, but it cannot help but be one. It is plausibility alone that is the cause of

---

[1] In his book *Le Hasard* [*Chance*], Emile Borel presents an analogous reasoning when he shows that one should not be surprised that three stars in a given constellation form the summit of a perfect equilateral triangle. One just has to know that there are only 23,000 possible angular groupings of three points that can be perceived differently, even if one used the most precise instruments. It follows that given the relative numerical infinity of constellations, it is very likely that one of them should present the form of a perfect equilateral triangle. Here one is dealing only with a probability, whereas in the case of the hair and the inhabitants of London, we are confronted with an ineluctable necessity.

this common yet unfounded assumption. If one had gone to the trouble of finding out the number of hairs on a man's head and the number of inhabitants of London, it is clear that the truth would have appeared clearly to the least-informed person. I would be happy if everyone took this prejudicial information into consideration in every circumstance. But this method—the scientific method—conflicts as much with laziness because of the work it requires as with good sense because of the frequent irrationality of its results. I am not afraid of pursuing the problem of overdetermination in the association of ideas with the utmost rigor. I would make it clear, therefore, that it is not a matter of *ideas* but of psychic elements whose nature is quite variable: memories, images, feelings, sensations, words, concepts. These elements are associated, let us repeat, contingently or contiguously. It seems to make more sense to me to say that they can be joined together either by the partial identity of their *intrinsic qualities* (which accounts for their association by resemblance) or by the equally partial superimposition of their *extrinsic conditions* (which explains their association by contiguity). Obviously the intermediaries by which they are brought together are also psychic elements capable of being associated as well as of associating. Thus one of the givens of the problem consists of the number of possible associations when one knows the total number of elements is *n*. The calculation shows that the sum *N* of the possible associations is so high in relation to *n,* especially when the latter is already fairly large, that this disproportion allows it to be considered in terms of a different dimension.[2] Because each element, far from being isolated, is also, by the very fact of its existence, in a direct or distant relationship with the others, it follows that each new actual or imagined

---

[2] One must take into consideration the direct association of these two elements, then the sum of possible associations through the intermediary of a single element, or $n-2$ combinations; then the sum of possible associations through the intermediary of two elements, or $2(n-3) + 2(n-4) + 2(n-5) + \ldots$ combinations; then through the intermediary of three elements, or $2(n-3)(n-2) + 2(n-3)(n-3) + 2(n-3)(n-4) \ldots$; and so on, up to and including, if one leaves aside the complex cases in which the same element would be used two or more times between the two elements being taken into

relationship is necessarily an overdetermination. In other words, there is a necessary overdetermination each time a relationship is set up, without any hitherto unknown or untested element being put into question. And because the number of virtual associations of this kind is practically infinite, there is a likelihood, bordering on a certainty, of a great many multiple overdeterminations.

Consequently, one would be wrong to consider unusual such cases as those that are analyzed in the present study and that, in fact, foreground an affective systematization of the overdetermined elements called ideograms. We have seen that among these representations some were the sole privilege of a subject because their lyrical capacity is only derived more or less from his or her personal adventures, whereas others, which owe their lyrical capacity above all to the very general evocative and emotive qualities that they contain, seem almost universal, founded as they are on primary phenomena that humans, irrespective of place or time, are capable of feeling.

We are obviously dealing here only with two limits, the very ones we ordinarily refer to as subjective and objective, and between these two are situated all ideograms that, given their representative and affective power, are made up of a variously proportional mix of these opposing qualities. This mix can hardly be conceived of as existing in a pure state, because thinking (which is part of it) finds it repugnant that within a single universe there should be differences in nature, that is, insurmountable oppositions. In fact, there is no reason at all to appeal to the (by no means negligible) existence of such coercion. It is so clear that to consider the distinction currently being put into question as irreducible is to refer to a philosophy that the mind likes to set apart,

---

consideration, the product $(n-3)(n-4)(n-5)\ldots$, which expresses the total number of possible associations of two elements through the intermediary of all the others, that is, through the intermediary of $n-2$ elements and that is of the order of n^{n-4}. The number N of all possible cases of associa- tion (except for the cases that are cyclical in nature) of two elements is provided by the sum of this series of expressions. It is easy to see how disproportionate it is to n.

for its own glory or humiliation, depending on the circumstances; a concept that in turn can only be based upon the experience of this *irreducibility,* unless through some vicious circle it is made to be based upon its own consequence. There are however, only experiences of the existent and the nonexistent here and now; there can be no question of the possible or impossible, and a fortiori of a possibility or an impossiblity. In other words, irreducibility is not a form of perception, but a category of understanding. I apologize for insisting so pedantically on the obvious, which everyone can experience and furthermore no one fabricates or is able to fabricate, but I felt it necessary to indicate the degree to which the irreducible distinction of the objective and the subjective constitutes a principled plea, because it is an opinion concerning a postulate, which in order to be valid must not only imply this postulate as such, but also propose it as an immediate, incontestable, unconditional, in short, absolute experience.

In this analysis I am in no way looking for some verbal, triumphant identification of the objective and the subjective. I am simply trying to restore the principle of continuity between the two poles; everywhere reason demonstrates the possiblity of this principle: experience demonstrates its existence and dialectics its necessity. I am the last person to underestimate the importance of their practical and even of their philosophical opposition, but on the other hand I am the first person to deny the legitimacy of the sort of transcendental dualism that one is often all too happy to transform it into through ever more abusive operations of simplification, of distribution, of distension, and of abstraction. For my part I attach the greatest importance to the *evidence of the senses.* No form of certainty appears more satisfying to me; none in any case is more elementary and more irreducible. The illusions of sight and of touch, all of the allegedly deceptive appearances, do not at all discredit this certainty in my eyes: one has only to consider these appearances in their place for it to be necessary to reckon with them as much as one would reckon with the most reliable testimonies, for—as we all know—an error is only an error insofar as it is taken to be the truth. I would hope for the strictest impartiality on this point. When one considers the problem of the imagination (that is, of putting into images), one notices that the physiological organ of sight—the eye—does not have to be taken into account. Indeed, the formation of an image on the retina in no way explains the phenomenon. For one has to assume a second eye that can perceive it, then a third eye to perceive the image formed on the retina of the second, and so on ad infinitum. Everyone knows, what is more, that images are perceived without the assistance of their eyes: dreams are the most striking example of this.

The first statements show that from perception to dreams, via representation and hallucination, *it is the faculty of the imagination alone that is at work, differentiated only by the diverse conditions that, one after another, specify its modes of action.*

Everything thus seems to be reduced to the faculty of perceiving in space. We are talking about the ideal space provided for us by an immediate experience, however brief, which above all has no say in the matter: this space is indeed ideal, for it in fact appears as an a priori form appropriate to both perceptions and hallucinations, whether one is awake or asleep. Its main quality is to be able to be simultaneously occupied by different representations: whence the experimental fact that several images can occupy the same place at the same time, as happens with the portion of the space located behind the door of a wardrobe with a mirror: in the same place there are the invisible real contents of the wardrobe and the visible reflected virtual image. Thus the *perception* in this instance gives a *virtual* image to which the *imagination* opposes a *real* content.[3] Now, imagination is often defined as a virtual perception, and perception as a real imagination; what is more, consciousness is no less often defined as a mirror reflecting the outside

---

[3] The composite character of space appears in an even more appreciable conflict when one looks out from a lighted room through a window into the dark outside: the tension between the virtual and the real only puts perception into question. They both use the same weapons to fight with, and depending on the situation, that is, the lighting, one or the other is the victor.

world. I will leave it to the reader to draw his or her own conclusions from these clever complications. I find this embarrassment and confusion far from displeasing: it is of course hardly a symptom, even less a prefiguration, and at most a sort of encouragement whose mythical nature does not escape me and whose significance seems to me to be of practically no consequence. I would not even mention it if the hypothesis of systematic overdetermination of the universe did not in addition seem to me to be connected to it in all of its aspects: from the rigorous determinism of the associations and syntheses of lyrical thinking to the existence of objectively moving ideograms.

However, the analyses in this book all tend to highlight, over and above this existence of elements with an objectively moving value and this multiple overdetermination of the universe, the rigorous lyrical determinism of the affective imagination. Does it not seem that they could be put to use together in order to provide the substance of some final resolution? It seems that the becoming aware of this systematization is nothing other than knowledge itself. But beyond that, it is the domain of metaphysical extrapolation, where it is hardly possible to bring to bear any concrete certainties. One can at most ask oneself what the effects of this perfect lucidity would be in this world of necessity and continuity. One has then to assume that someone who has gained access to the complete knowledge of one's mind's necessity would be unable to doubt that it coincides with the necessity of the universe. Fusing perfectly with the necessity of the universe, the mind's necessity would at the same time be absorbed in it. It is difficult to imagine what exteriority, what antinomy would remain for such a being. And who cannot see that salvation lies beyond any distiction, or else it lies nowhere at all?

It is a question now, even more pressing than these bold speculations, of an undertaking that is far more humble, crude, and compromising: This is the rigorous pursuit, taking into account the lyrical demands of affectivity and of thinking, of some approximate lucidity, for which there is nothing to be done but to learn the thankless patience of the scholar.

114

SUPPORTING AND
SUPPLEMENTARY DOCUMENTS

I

NOTE ON THE SCIENTIFIC ACTIVITY OF AUGUST STRINDBERG AROUND 1896[1]

Given that it is at the present time difficult to consult the text of *Inferno,* a book that has become almost impossible to find, I think it would be helpful to reproduce the most important section of the chapter that Strindberg devoted to the study of the *Acherontia atropos.* Its subtitle is "Essay on Rational Mysticism," and it begins with a few remarks on the coloring of the scales of certain fish, after which the author writes the following:

> *I had never seen the Death's-head or* Acherontia
> atropos, *the moth with the human skull on its corselet,*
> *when I bought it from a naturalist. Astonished to see the*
> *image more distinctly marked than I had expected, I set*
> *about studying this animal.*
> *And I read that the Bretons say it prophesies death. It*
> *lets out a plaintive cry when it is frightened: the caterpillar*

---

[1] See chapter 2, p. 20.

117

feeds on Solanaceae, *jasmin, and thorn apples,* Datura stramonium *and forms a chrysalis deep down in the earth in an agglutinated shell.*

There were many comparisons here with death: the announcement of death, the lugubrious song, the mortal potion of the stramonium, the burial of the caterpillar. . . .

Reader: I am not superstitious by nature, but when, after having gathered this information, I came across Réaumur, the famous physician and insect expert who recounts that the Death's-head appears periodically, and especially during times of great epidemics, please understand that I have given a lot of thought to the habits of the moth and its relationship to its macabre markings.

First of all, the caterpillar feeds on solanine and daturine, two vegetable alkaloids related to morphine, but also very close to deadly poisons, to ptomaines and leucomaines. These poisons give off the odor of jasmin, rose, and musk, among others.

There are plants called corpse-plants (arum, stapelia, orchis etc.) which smell of corpses, have a corpse-like color and attract insects that feed on carrion.

Is it not logical that the Death's-head should visit the places where epidemics are rampant and where there are decomposing bodies?

Moreover, solanine is a narcotic poison. Is this why the butterfly sleeps during the day and the night, and only vegetates and propagates at dawn and at dusk?

And daturine contains the two alkaloids atropine and hyoscyamine; the atropine in the deadly nightshade dilates the pupils or at least makes daylight intolerable. Is this the cause of the crepuscular habits of the Death's-head, and of its fearing the sun, nonetheless forced, by the soporific effects of the hyoscyamine, to sleep at night? It appears so. Now, hyoscyamine, the poison in henbane, brings with it

118

the additional inconvenience that the victim perceives objects as being larger than they actually are (megalopia).

We can imagine, then, a Death's-head led astray by its deceptive sense of smell to cemeteries, to refuse dumps, to scaffolds and gallows, where it looks at human skulls that are tremendously enlarged, and we may well ask ourselves whether this could act upon the nerves of a moth that is impressionable to the point of emitting plaintive cries when it is teased, a butterfly doubly delirious from being in heat and from the intoxicating venom of henbane; a double intoxication equal to hysteria.

In *Sylva Sylvarum* (German translation, Georg Müller Verlag, München) we can find a rather different study of the same subject, one more complete and less rigorous. Finally, there is a third version, in *Botanical Gardens* (Göteborg: Heldlund, 1896, in Swedish).

In a letter to his editor, Strindberg presents the outline for his complete work as follows (2 April 1896):

SYLVA SYLVARUM

    I. In the Botanical Gardens. The sighs of the stones.
    II. Indigo and aqua-fortis. Sulphur at the Sorbonne.
    III. Antibarbarus.
    IV. Introduction to a unitarian chemistry.
    V. The violet of the Alps. The nerves of a plant. The Death's-head moth.
    VI. Optics. Spectral analysis. Theory of colors.
    VII. Astronomy.

So it was a systematic study, the very one whose author characterizes it as follows in *Inferno:* "This book is one of great disorder and of infinite coherence." He managed only a very disorderly completion of his plan, publishing several chapters in one pamphlet, then grouping them differently in another, such that each study appears in several places. One would do well, if one wanted to clarify this confusion a little, to refer to the two volumes in the German edition of the complete works entitled *Natur-Trilogie* and *Antibarbarus*, and to the bibliography put together by Emil Schering in the first of these volumes.

I only quote this study on the *Acherontia atropos* as an example. It is not the only one of its kind. There is also one on the *Cyclamen europeum* that is much less interesting, in chapter 5 of *Inferno*.

Strindberg's activity around this time also seems quite disjointed. In addition to his countless chemistry experiments, which periodically led him back to the hospital, he undertook others (these were optical experiments) that seemed to him to prove that "the sun is itself a virtual image" (*Samlade Skrifter,* Stockholm, 1921, vol. 27, p. 373). He refutes all the arguments that state that the earth is round (pp. 374-381). He points out the identity of the characteristic numbers of the planets (distance from the sun, diameter, density, revolution time) and of the numbers of the metals (atomic weight, density, freezing point, specific heat), which, according to medieval astrology, correspond to the former (pp. 433-440). In *Inferno* he is more immediate and more concrete. In his introduction, Marcel Réja characterizes this work as follows:

> *Starting out from reality and clinging energetically to it, as he sees it, Strindberg connects the facts together one after another according to perfectly unexpected laws, and ends up with his system of what he considers as the world, completely foreign to what we are accustomed to considering as reality. . . . He combines into a disquieting system what we systematically eliminate from the domain of our attention.* (pp. 7-8)

I can only subscribe to the intention, if not the execution. Consequently, what I am doing in the present study is to take up the enterprise again.

II

NOTE ON THE MYTHIC SIGNIFICANCE OF THE NOVEL,
BY PIERRE BENOIT OF THE ACADÉMIE FRANÇAISE,
ENTITLED ATLANTIDA

I mentioned that I was struck by the mythic dimension of this book. While reading by chance the very unsatisfactory articles by C. G. Jung collected under the title *Papers on Analytical Psychology* a short time ago, that is to say with no conscious intention or premeditation, I was pleased to note that the character Antinea was in fact quoted in them as representing the archetypal woman, that is, as the projection of a primitive image belonging to the collective unconscious and ultimately being nothing more than a product of the latter.[1] This could, it seems to me, explain the unusual kind of extra-literary success that the work of Pierre Benoit has enjoyed and continues to enjoy. There is no question—and this has now become very clear—that the author was trying to appeal to a well-read audience, which is also, at least in my eyes, an irrevocable judgment of him. It is a fact that among these same readers *Atlantida* has met with a marked and scornful hostility, although ordinary readers of serialized novels have greeted it favorably.

---

[1] It is in my opinion not an insignificant confirmation that the subject analyzed by Dr. Jacques Lacan in his thesis *De la psychose paranoïaque dans ses rapports avec la personnalité* [*On Paranoid Psychosis in its Relation to Personality*] (Paris: Seuil Points, 1980) identifies with Pierre Benoit's heroines. The author twice quotes this sentence, which also happens to be one of the most characteristic, that the patient uses to try to describe how the imaginary creatures get into the system of her delirium: "It was as if they bounced off my imagination," she confessed.

This is, however, only of marginal interest. The fact that Jung should be able to account for the main traits of the character Antinea on the basis of his hypothesis seems to me even more expedient. Indeed, it seems natural that a collective and ancestral conception of women should culminate in the projection of an image devoid of any maternal features, that is, exclusively erotic and feminine, and thereby appearing, however slightly, as a prostitute or as an enigma. From Jung's short analysis I want to retain above all the fact that she provides an interesting explanation of the "genealogical tendency" that he has noted both in *Atlantida* and in *She* by Rider Haggard, the two books he uses as examples. Thus there would be a conflation of the ideogrammatic themes of the femme fatale and of the dynastic feeling that I was led to talk about at different points in my study, and of whose connection I was so unconscious that when I was analyzing the concept of dynasty I did not even remember that each time I recommended *Atlantida* to someone, I absolutely insisted that chapter 13 be skipped, which insinuates that Antinea is not the authentic descendant of Neptune and of Atlas, as is proved at length in chapter 9, but the daughter of a Polish adventurer and a working-class Parisian girl. Moreover, I had explicitly underlined this connection in the following text written a long time ago now, which I thought of as a speech uttered by the night, even though it can scarcely be related to anything other than a mythical woman like Antinea, an aberration that is furthermore overdetermined in several ways:[2]

> *He had expected too much from love. He would only*
> *have needed a decisive satisfaction for such a great desire,*

---

[2] In particular through lines such as these:

> *It is the woman who is loved*
> *because of the Night*
> *And those who have known her*
> *talk of her softly*

taken from the remarkable play by Villiers de l'Isle-Adam entitled *Conte d'amour* [*Tale of Love*] (Oeuvres complètes, vol. 2, pp. 353-362), which would be worthy of lengthy analysis that could not fail to be instructive.

and when in an impartial light, which was now hers, she reflected upon the uncertainty of mortals, if she did not feel it necessary to judge this uncertainty to be vain and a hundred times emptier than their anguish itself, she at least congratulated herself on having crossed the borderline of their dominion.

She would not, however, describe her own dominion to him. Suffice for him to know that all in it was solemn and royal, in a profound sense, and that once he had received a letter whose stamp bore a name unknown to all geographers, he would better understand that she comes from the dead. He would have to tremble henceforth when he thought of the possible anonymity of telephone calls.

It was in order to get closer to him that she had at first not wanted to discuss the noble things that she was eager to talk to him about. For several consequences, equally to her credit, resulted from the fact that she both commanded his attention and was out of his reach.

Others might have thought that she had escaped from mirrors or, because of her own obscurity, had descended from some boreal star; and that the problem of her own origins was now of little importance to the serenity of her admiration. She herself had never deemed men's desires compatible with the magnificence of her body, nor their praise with the loftiness of her pride. Thus tyrants, whose cruelty appalls history, would shudder at her cruelty if they had known how murderous it was. Indeed, it did not seem as if the presence of living beings was an obstacle to her wiles, so peremptory was the sovereign indifference of her eyes.

What is more, the corpses taken out of cathedrals after she had gone by could have informed him about the nature of her habits. Her palace had no windows because it was made entirely of crystal. How had he not guessed this?

Encouraged by this intersection, which was both unexpected and decisive, I was tempted to identify what Jung called "archetypes" with what I had called "objective ideograms." But it was not long before I realized that one can hardly superimpose the two concepts. In fact, I am quite inclined to agree with Jung that there exists a "terrestrial conditioning of the soul" and that, as a result, there are fundamental images born out of the representative possibilities of the collective unconscious (even though one would have to come to an agreement about the meaning of the latter expression) that are affected by, for example, the diurnal path of the sun, the phases of the moon, and the idea that a child has of its mother and an adolescent of a woman. Yet these archetypes are human fantasies, with universal value it is true, and can consequently lay no claim to the materiality of those elements, independent from man, whose existence I have attempted to demonstrate and of which I offered a model in the praying mantis. Consequently, Jung's archetype, because it has no concrete objectivity, in no way raises the question of the natural overdetermination to which this work is primarily devoted.

III

*CRITICAL RESERVATIONS ON MOST OF THE WORKS AND
EXPERIMENTS UNDERTAKEN UNTIL NOW ON THE
ASSOCIATION OF IDEAS*

As has been noted for a long time now (See E. Claparède, *L'Association des idées* [*The Association of Ideas*], Doin, 1903), the usual concern when it comes to the association of ideas is to use it in order to explain, rather than to explain it itself. Several authors have nonetheless broached this problem. Unfortunately, they have generally done so in such artificial conditions that their subjects have been forced to adopt procedures that are no less artificial, merely repeating, for example, the names of the objects they had in front of them (the proportion of such repetitions was always higher than 33%), or, being content to think in terms of series, reciting one after another the names of trees, kitchen utensils, furniture, great men, and so on that they remembered: *such that in actual fact they would substitute in the one case perception, and in the other, memory, for the imagination whose elementary forms people wanted to study.*

Elsewhere, A. Binet (*Etude expérimentale de l'intelligence* [*Experimental Study of Intelligence*], Paris, 1903, p. 23) is forced to renounce previous works because they always deal exclusively with associations of words while paying no attention to their content (unless one is asked complementary questions), and about which it is not even known whether they correspond to a latent concrete image or to some barely specified object, which is, in any case, devoid of any particular attributes. In fact, researchers have often tried to eliminate not only the affective meaning, but even the intellectual meaning of the elements.

Thus Ebbinghaus experimented with 2,300 syllables, which he put together and chose himself in such a way that they are nothing but sounds. Th. L. Smith, Müller, and Pilzecker (and even Scripture with mediated associations) proceeded in the same way.

It is easy to understand why, having abstracted the question from all reality, these authors should have arrived at very uninteresting results, which, in any case, are absolutely useless from my standpoint, according to which it would be desirable with every object to take into account the entire history of the individual who is making the associations.

It would at the very least have been necessary to look at long associations obtained in conformity with procedures and in circumstances that had been just as well defined, and of which the "waking reveries" of the sexual pervert studied by R. de Saussure (*Revue Française de Psychanalyse* 3rd year, no. 4, pp. 675-680) seems to me to provide a good example.[1] We can easily recognize the ideogrammatic themes that make them up and the obsessional ideograms that systematize the whole. Hence the theme of bifurcation illustrated by the foot, and by things that open, and suck: flowers, fists, octopuses, sea anemones, and so on, which are also symbols of the vagina; the phallic theme with the tower, the white column, the elephant, the spinning top; the theme of hermaphrodism with the snake and the elephant's trunk, which can both "wrap itself around and become erect" at the same time, can become a sucker, a tentacle, a mouth, and a sexual organ.

It is rare to find records of nondirected associations of ideas. It is odd that one exists precisely in Strindberg's *Inferno,* in chapter 7,

---

[1] One ought also to mention the attempt made by Baron Ch. Mourre in his study "La Volonté dans le rêve" [Will in Dreams"] (Revue Philos., 1903, pp. 508-559 and 634 ff.). After having tried to define psychic automatism by successive eliminations, this author published a forced chain of associations and tried without much luck to interpret it (p. 645). This chain is reproduced by Yves Delage in his book *Le rêve* [*Dreams*] (Nantes, 1920, pp. 214-215), and he prefaces it with this explanatory principle, which will be of interest here:

To emerge into consciousness and to become fully manifest, these

"Study of Funerals." I will reproduce it here with the passage immediately preceding it, in which the author recounts the circumstances of
its composition:

> *For eight months I have been observing the most beauti-*
> *ful monument in the cemetery. It is a composite work, a*
> *sarcophagus, a sepulchre, a vault, a mausoleum, a ceno-*
> *taph, an urn, in the finest Ancient Roman style. Sculpted*
> *out of pink granite, it bears no inscription, and I have for a*
> *long time confused it with the broken column, "the mon-*
> *ument to memory, in memory of those who have none."*
>
> *What secret is hidden there? A proud modesty that*
> *obliges the visitor to question, or asks about what he*
> *already knows.*
>
> *The other day, preoccupied by my solitary thoughts, I*
> *stopped in front of a sign indicating the name of the inter-*
> *secting avenue where that magnificent anonymous person*
> *had erected his monument, Chauveau-Lagarde Avenue. A*
> *sudden glow illuminated my brain, and then the night of*
> *oblivion descended again. As I looked at the sarcophagus,*
> *red with coagulated blood that had a yellowish tint to it,*
> *I repeated: Chauveau-Lagarde, just as you repeat the*
> *unknown name of someone you have known.*
>
> *The avenue probably owed its name to this Chauveau-*
> *Largarde . . . Chauveau-Lagarde . . . Chauveau-*
> *Lagarde . . . yes, Chauveau-Lagarde Street! Chauveau-*

---

embryonic ideas grow actively,
assisted by their residual energy,
and are passively drawn out by the
associative link that connects them
to the idea present at the time in
the conscious mind. The chances
of their success in forcing open the
front door are measured by the

product of these two independent
factors. (p. 212)

*Lagarde Street behind the Madeleine! The mysterious
murder of an old woman in 1893, in Chauveau-Lagarde
Street . . . red with coagulated blood . . . the two
assassins were never caught!*

*Accustomed to observing everything that happens in my
soul, I remember having been gripped by an unusual terror,
while images crowded each other in complete disorder, like
the thoughts of a madman. I saw Louis XVI's counsel, with
the guillotine behind him; I saw a large river flanked by
green hills, a young mother taking a little girl for a walk
along the river, then a monastery with an altar retable
by Velasquez; I am in Sarzeau in the Lesage Hotel where
there is a Polish edition of the* Diable boiteux [The Lame
Devil]; *I am behind the Madeleine, in Chauveau-Lagarde
Street . . . ; I am at the Bristol Hotel in Berlin where I dis-
patch a telegram to Laroyer at the London Hotel. I am in
Saint-Cloud where a woman in a Rembrandt hat is writh-
ing with the pain of childbirth; I am at the Regency Café,
where the Köln cathedral is on view, made out of raw
sugar . . . and where the wine waiter claims that it was
built by Monsieur Ranelagh and Marshal Berthier . . .*

What was this? I have no idea! a hurricane of memories, of
dreams evoked by a tombstone, chased away by cowardice.

The analysis would have had to examine documents such as these,
even though it could hardly be carried out by anyone except their
author.

SUPPLEMENTARY INQUIRY INTO THE TWO LINES
ANALYZED IN CHAPTER 4 AND TAKEN FROM
RALENTIR TRAVAUX *BY ANDRÉ BRETON,*
RENÉ CHAR, AND PAUL ELUARD
(EDITIONS SURRÉALISTES, 1930)

The women who in love hear the wind pass through the
poplar trees
The women who in hate are more taut than praying
mantises.

It seemed to me of interest to verify the emotional capacity of these two lines with their author, because I had so many reasons to consider them as very generally applicable as I did the lyrical power of the ideograms associated with them.

The texts of *Ralentir Travaux* were composed in the following manner: each participant, after having written several lines, would read them to the next person who would then immediately write his own. It was André Breton who wrote the lines in question. So I asked him what memories were evoked by each of the words he used when writing them, without being anymore precise about the purpose of my investigation and without letting him know of my hypothesis concerning the existence of ideograms that had an objective lyrical value. This is what he associates with the words:

Poplar tree: a tree that played an important role in his childhood in Lorraine with his father, so it was a "phallic symbol," he said; there were wide roads bordered by poplars. "I might add that they were the only good thing there." At fifteen he frequently imagined following these roads at dusk with the woman he would love interminably; such walks seemed much more desirable to him "than, for example, being alone with this woman in an enclosed place." The word *poplar* by itself also seemed "very beautiful" to him, he said.

Wind: first a literary memory, that of a line from Rimbaud, "But how the wind is wholesome,"[1] which he associates with a particular way of saying, imitating a great wind blowing, and taken up by Breton in *Mont de Piété* [*Pawnshop*], "which is something he never does." He also hates the wind, and for him the most ridiculous situation is to try to read a newspaper or a letter when it is windy (a permanent dislike of his, it seems; he had already told me this on a completely unrelated occasion).

Praying mantis: the normal attraction to the name and the habits of this insect, which is something he has felt for a long time. Thus, in 1924 he planned to start up a press whose distinctive ·mark, to be reproduced on all its books, was a drawing he commissioned Max Ernst to do specially, representing a praying mantis in the spectral position.[2] He also remembers that J. Viot, who was "deeply shocked," told him that Arthur Cravan's widow (or perhaps Mela Muter, whom Breton is confusing her with), pitted praying mantises against each other and against other insects. He always found the mantis very beautiful, especially its "triangular head"; he was not disappointed when he saw one for the first time, in fact quite the opposite, which is not the case most of the time. This insect interests him so much that he had a "dried" specimen of one in one of his desk drawers (he had first said "mummified," a slip that goes a long way toward confirming the latent

---

[1] A. Rimbaud, "Blackcurrant River," in *Collected Poems*, trans. Oliver Bernard (Harmondsworth: Penguin, 1962).

[2] This drawing is featured in the program notes to the film *L'Age d'Or [The Golden Age]*, p. 3.

identification whose great likelihood I mentioned when pointing out the extraordinarily anthropomorphic appearance of the mantis).

As one can see, these answers, particularly as concerns the two main ideograms — the poplar tree and the praying mantis—strictly corroborate my analysis and contribute to proving for themselves the objective lyrical value of the image in *Ralentir Travaux*.

V

ON TWO MANTIS SUBSTITUTES

Mantids are unevenly spread over the surface of the planet. In particular, they require a warm or temperate climate. But it does not seem necessary to dwell on their rarity or absence in a given region; there is no shortage of animal species that can stand in for them in terms of their representative function.

I would like to draw attention to two of them: the spider, which like the mantis devours its male; and the crab, which is also autotomic and cannibalistic. It seems conclusive to me that these two animals are precisely the most impressive, and they play such a large part in mythology and folklore that A. de Gubernatis was led to devote a whole chapter to each of them in his work *Zoological Mythology* (1:14 and 3:2). This work, despite being very comprehensive, is useless: it was written in the heroic age of solar madness and is consequently just a series of often ridiculous distortions.

I will mention several facts taken from elsewhere as examples.

The crab is featured on coins from Agrigento. It is worshipped, among other places, on the coast of Mexico, as Garcilaso de la Vega reports in the sixteenth century in his *Comentarias Reales*. Elsewhere E. H. Man (*Journal of the Anthropological Institute,* Nov. 1882) writes that the natives of the Andaman Islands (in the Bay of Bengal) believe that certain men become crabs. Last, but not least, the crab (Cancer) is one of the signs of the zodiac.

There is little to choose between the spider and the crab: the natives of the Gold Coast consider the spider the divinity that created the universe, whereas the natives of the Banks Islands rank it along with their divine hero Qat as one of the Superior Spirits or Vuis (see Codrington, *The Melanesians, Studies in their Anthropology and Folklore,* 1891; Lang, *Myth, Ritual, and Religion,* p. 342). In the Upanishads, Brahman is compared to the spider secreting and resorbing its thread (*Mandaka Upanishad,* vol. I, p. 7). A woman who was possessed, and who was locked up in Charenton, vomited live spiders (see J. Bizouard, *Des rapports de l'homme avec le démon* [*The Relationship between Man and the Devil*], Paris, 1863, vol. 3, p. 584); Magdeleine Bavent, in the convent prison cell where she was wasting away, swallowed them in vain in order to die (see Michelet, *La Sorcière* [*The Witch*], vol. 2, p. 8). One should also recall the famous anecdotes of Pelisson raising spiders in prison and of Spinoza taking pleasure seeing them eat the flies he fed to them. The case of Odilon Redon insistently painting spiders with women's heads seems to me to reveal the significance one ought to attribute to these kinds of obsessions.

These few facts are intended only to give a quick overview of the appreciable series of correspondences that appear to sustain the relationship established earlier among the mantis, the spider, and the crab. There is more decisive evidence. Indeed, the relationship has had popular confirmation for a long time now, in a form that, even if elementary, is nonetheless explicit: a variety of *crab,* also a symbol of wisdom in antiquity, is commonly called a *spider* crab, and a closely related shellfish (of the lesser sand eel genus) has no other name than a *mantis* shrimp.

Of course, the mythology of the mantis is not exhausted by the few facts recounted in chapter 5, where the question is dealt with only in relation to the problem of lyrical objectivity. I hope to return to it in the near future as an independent question, using the Romanian legends, according to which the *calugarita* (praying mantis) is the devil's daughter, the remarks by Hesiod in his Orphic poems on Pandora's enigmatic character, and those of the Atharva-Veda on the Krytà and the Visakanyà, artificial poison-virgins related at once to golems and to succubi, and, more generally, using as my point of departure all the sanguinary female phantoms of ancient myths and of present-day folklore that appear in dreams during the night, and even more so in the raw and blinding light of midday, the spectral hour.[1]

[1] For further facts, see J. C. Frazer, *The Golden Bough,* 3rd edition, Macmillan, 1915. On the spider: vol. 1, p. 152; vol. 8, p. 236 ff.; vol. 9, p. 381. On the crab: vol. 1, p. 289; vol. 9, p. 103. It is especially interesting to note that the two animals are often used for the same purpose, namely, "to extract vicious propensities" (vol. 9, p. 34).

RISK OF LIFE
Text Illustrating a Certain Stage of Development of
Ideogrammatic Themes

I felt I had to quote the long text that follows in its entirety. It was written not so long ago, and if it is unfortunately not completely free of naïveté and of literature, it is still a relatively valid and comprehensive document of my preoccupations at the time and contains in its lyrical sections allusions to almost all the ideogrammatic themes I have had occasion to mention in the course of my analysis. This being the case, instead of quoting short fragments from it here and there, it seemed to me preferable to reproduce all of it, facilitating the task of coordination for the reader with an appropriate system of references. So I am, in fact, providing a complementary crystallization whose intersections with the others reinforce my propositions on the multiple networks of overdetermination and shows, considered in isolation because of its interweaving of theoretical and lyrical elements, to what extent the concepts and representations perform the same emblematic function with respect to the affective imagination and the passional complexes.

It did not seem to me useful, moreover, to analyze the text itself, even though the work is less difficult than it appears; it contains—even in the passages that are apparently the product of the most disordered imagination—a considerable number of allusions to precise and easily appreciable events. But a study of this kind, duplicating the previous ones, would hardly have offered an interest proportionate to its length. The same is true for a text of similar inspiration, "Le Second Epithalame [The Second Epithalamium]," which I published in *Cahiers du*

Sud, April 1933, pp. 270-277, and do not feel is worth reproducting here.

RISK OF LIFE

Speech on Lyrico-Erotic Necessity

I have very strongly felt the necessity of a certain gran-diloquence, one which has a qualitative and symptomatic value, in order to tolerate a speech being deprived of the tone and the frame implied by its specific content. One could choose, for this content, an extremely disdainful way of expressing oneself—as a young technician, for example, would pronounce the truth, or what he insolently offers as such, on a question that is one of the most remarkable in its complexity and uncertainty. If in addition one agrees to bear in mind that the orator speaks at dusk in a place as completely and obviously devoid of interest as the Place du Théâtre Français, but no less explicitly suspect, it will per-haps be a little more difficult to deflect the following remarks away from their inadmissible goal.

I hope, first of all, that it will be recognized with good grace that the generally sordid representation that men have of death is too polite to be honest, and that its so very careful abstraction works, if not to make it reassuring, then at least to make it lose its thickness and density. It is indeed understandable, without needing to belabor the point, that between the IDEA of death, and life pure and simple, the advantage ends up with the latter, and that the concept of destruction is no match for the so cleverly named survival instinct. Yet we think that it is not too much to demand that one should propose (the word is, if one thinks about it for any length of time, truly laughable),

138

propose then, that death no longer be regarded as an ideal possibility which there will always be time to take care of the next day, but as an immediately present and imperious force, of the same nature as gravity and, like gravity, directed towards the center of the earth; this is moreover its only perverse aspect when one thinks, along with the polisher of glass lenses, that the only virtue resides in the precisely inverse force that compels human beings to persevere in their being.

It is in the devastated countryside of love that death can be lived and breathed daily: metamorphoses as one leaves the towns; —man's delicious fatigue when he notices his gestures, which have become more and more scarce, only long after they have been performed, in and of themselves, by virtue of their own weight and, so to speak, of their own authority; —the wonderful fatigue of someone who all day long, on the pretext of walking, has never stopped going up and down imaginary steps that are incontestably metaphysical and erotic and that isolated him, in the sense in which electricians understand this word, from life—this morning he had a dramatic prefiguration of this isolation when, for the first time, he saw the gigantic sheet metal cage of the CITÉ subway stop, with its cluttered mass of elevators and stairways, apparently so clear and symmetrical; —the irreparable fatigues, finally, of those who cross immense, deserted, useless fields as they follow the interminable junction canals thanks to which long barges, so often burdened down with openly fraudulent and provocative cargo, easily pass through forbidden locks, and bring the silvery germs of an incurable leprosy to the only regions that have not yet been contaminated.

Of course it is in the devastated countryside of passion that death can be lived and breathed daily: who would not see in this weariness the very mask of an inertia that is always on the brink of violence, and that is only waiting for love in order to rush into it head first?

★

It is only too clear, moreover, that when love and death have been brought together, it has usually been by a kind of literary and allegedly poetic inflation, whose principle is abject, and whose application is even more so.[1] *But it is nonetheless necessary to denounce the fact that the conscious or unconscious misrecognition of their terrible alliance allows a permanent fraudulence to occupy an area that is too precious and moving for it to be suffered there, even on the pretext that* life *has* everything *to gain by it.*

I'm sure that many people in their experience have come across these signs which put everything back in its place, and I myself will not hesitate to invoke, as a particularly overwhelming testimony to the intimate complicity between love and death, this dream where I had to die at the admirable hands of the woman I loved. I had finally learned, although not to my surprise, that she was the one who had been chosen to murder me by the Inaccessible Shadow (sovereign of the world, according to a novel in the weekly illustrated children's paper, L'Intrépide [The Intrepid One]*, who lived in the heart of Tibet in the City of the Ice*

---

[1] In my case it is a matter of a deep-seated and, in a sense, primitive identification, as attested to by this text written (from a dream) before any experience of, and even before any knowledge of, a sexual nature:

> *The room was long, wide, and deserted, and ended inappropriately in a huge staircase that disappeared from view as you looked up. And high up on the top step was a woman dressed in white. He was trembling. But she was already coming down, and on each step her leg was becoming uncovered. He was trembling. She was near him and had long since taken off her mask. He was wrong*

Phantoms) and who had only been granted two days to accomplish her mission.[2] *It was not long before I discovered, in the shady area around the tent of a travelling circus,* this woman to whom I had always abandoned my right and my power to defend my life when I was face to face with her. I was already strangling her when she begged me, her eyes full of tears of love, to let myself instead be strangled by her, this being inexplicably the price of my existence. So, miraculously freed because of my simple and absolute mental consent, and just far enough away from me that she could reach me with her rigid and tense arms, she began to mortally grip my throat, and through the terrible suffering of dying I heard her explaining to me until I *awoke,* that is to say until my death, *in an extraordinarily passionate voice that I had never known in her before, the depth of her love and the sublimity of its present fulfilment. It is really quite strange that I have entirely forgotten these magnificent and indisputable revelations, but I am ready to testify until the end of time that they were the unique and true solution to the problem, and that it is a shame they were so irremediably buried on the other side of a border that a passport with a photograph will never be enough to get across.*

I feel that the content of this dream is sufficiently rigorous and dialectical and, especially in relation to me, sufficiently exact and expected, *that any commentary, at*

---

to be astonished by this. He was reeling before her moist eyes, into which he was both afraid and eager to fall. He placed his two arms in the Queen's two hands as a gift. She was now naked and his was nothing but a shadow that had faded into her.

[2] A further personification of the mythical female sovereign, see chapter 3.

least here, seems superfluous; I will leave it up to the spe-
cialists, then, to appreciate the details as they see fit, while
I point out in the meantime to their benevolent attention
that I feel with a very special and by no means indifferent
emotion the exchange of murders so lovingly performed on
the one hand, and on the other the fact, by no means iso-
lated, that waking up took the place of death and annihila-
tion. As for the contradiction that, on my own testimony, I
always remember perfectly the words I listen to or utter in
dreams, but as it happens do not remember those I heard
in this dream, far from inferring that they were not as
decisively important as I felt them to be at the time, one
could instead legitimately see in this further proof of their
inestimable value, if one considers that from the perspec-
tive of the famous survival instinct such a mysterious lapse
of memory has every chance of being providential.

In any case, whether or not because of these deep deter-
minations the organization of life necessitates such naïvely
accommodating gaps in memory, and whether or not it
can allow the archipelago of dreams in privileged circum-
stances to be anything other than a succession of reefs, one
would have to attribute to this organization the desperate
fact that in contemporary society it is contradictory to live
and to attain complete lucidity with respect to the most
immediate and anguishing questions, the only ones, above
all, against which no criticism can prevail; this lucidity is
also corrosive and cruel as well, like the cold, and far from
bringing them any remedy or answer by making the lyrical
and erotic necessity that fends them off or, more exactly,
that strips them bare, into something blinding, it will only
ultimately render the slightest disobedience to its merciless
imperatives inexcusable. This happily and wildly contin-
uous determinism, which it is only now possible to perceive
sporadically, but which still must be considered henceforth

142

as the only system of morals that is absolutely founded, and the one that is by far the most implacable and strictest, will only be able to manifest itself in to its true power and extent thanks to the Revolution. Once the psychological and other explanations have been denounced, it will be possible to revise more effectively than at the present time the unilateral conception of life, which is here being put into question.

Until then, apart from the elementary and often disappointing obligations that love makes manifest, indifference seems to be, all things considered, the right conduct, *since it is obviously through this conduct alone that one has any chance of attaining the lyrical necessity in which we have to hope to be able to one day set, so tightly that the blood squirts out, our flesh, our screams, our hands, our eyes.*

It is the least disinterested mind in the world that is speaking: and by indifference should be understood nothing but the surrender of the will to live, of knowing how to live, to the obsessive positive or negative demands of the many focal points of fear or of desire in which everyone has been able since childhood to accumulate the most equivocal secretions: for one person it is snakes of marble and gold; for another — (for me) — furry, bold, and gluttonous spiders; for a third person, sponges or some other such completely unexpected object.[3] It is highly recommended in the beginning to focus one's attention a little

---

[3] The first conception of objective ideograms.

more on those precious residues with the easily accessible goal of holding in check, before anything else, the intellectual and artistic desires of various kinds that prevent man from acting in the ways in which he is most violently solicited to do so. This being the case, indifference can only end up in a de facto *failure of understanding when dealing with all of the abstract oppositions, not only those of the usefulness/harmfulness type, but also those, hardly more valid even within the confines of a restricted experience, of happiness and unhappiness, of sleeping and being awake. It aims then, first and foremost, to transform life into a* fall.[4] *Sometimes it is a slow fall into anxiety, sometimes a sudden one into vertigo, and its first effect is to make the disastrous notion of attenuating circumstances forever inconceivable. Nothing, at any rate, is more likely to convince the sceptics of its heterogeneity, which is radical to the extent that within one and the same world it is possible to distinguish unconditionally two things about love and death. It will seem insufficient to simply oppose their demands, when a less easily soluble contradiction or, to state it a better way, one whose resolution depends less on the right or wrong desire to live, will have been highlighted by the certainty that love is only defined as the passionate pursuit of a limit, when on the contrary life only goes on insofar as it is an interval, a measurable interval between birth and death.*

---

[4] This can be related to the psychasthenic theme, chapters 4 and 7.

One can understand now why people are so intent on making birth and death into two precise and well-determined immobilities, instead of perceiving them as indefinitely receding asymptotes that never meet. Civil status is blatantly malicious: man's birth is nothing more than the horizon of his memory, the variable point of the past where it runs up against the outside darkness. This is why the exploration, conquest and effective occupation of the unlimited premnesic time of life should figure prominently on the list of preliminary ambitions. Similarly desire and lucidity pursue death. For their indefinite demand for what is to come, to which we are fond of attaching great importance, as we do with prime numbers, is only divisible by itself, twin mirrors giving a very unreassuring image, to tell the truth, but an exact one, just as an obsession can be exact: a sensory presumption.[5]

At any rate, it is enough that memory and desire, if one is committed to them, should in turn be falls. Falls: anyone who, having reached the top of a staircase in the dark, has thought they had one more step to climb and who has let themselves fall a few derisory centimeters, but with complete confidence and with all their weight, and who in sleep has felt this same sensation which it would not be an exageration to call frantic, will understand the terrible meaning to which this word is entitled. Likewise, the moment that love is more than a pleasant pastime for people who are

---

[5] Here we have a true ideogram. I generally cannot go into a café without being multiplied by one of those sets of parallel mirrors. Nothing disturbs me as much as the kind of fog that finally drowns the view of the reflections. I still pay the greatest attention to the theme of crossing through the mirror and even to the most ordinary phenomena of reflection. See Conclusion, p. 109.

bored, the moment it devalues secondary determinations such as the lives of the lovers, and replaces them in a sense with its own catastrophic becoming, these lovers are less than the hallucinated travellers of a mad train and, to put it bluntly, they can only fall. It is true that since their destiny is inevitable, they have all the more freedom to reflect upon it, travellers of love.

Far from the solar sponges and from the variable brightness of the madrepore as it unloads its buccaneers, it was the first time they had acquiesced and were at rest. For others it was the triumphal joy with its additional angle, adolescents crying in their beds for want of women, and the acclimation of harmful animals, but theirs is the calm of bread, the calm of the celebration of national holidays in the redeemed provinces, the calm of the day and of chance words. In their drunkenness they had trouble raising their cups up to their clay lips; they let their hands wander over a large nearby heap of daggers, of flowers and of jewels, and their hands fished out at random, as slowly as a phonograph, a blade or a bracelet that was too heavy, marvel of water, perfect laws of oriental greed, farewells the length of transcontinental express trains. They had invented chances and fates, and had allowed themselves to be caught in their own traps when they had become independent enough from them to ever free themselves from them. And the consequences had been disastrous.

---

[6] See the lines by Rimbaud:
And in order to compose
Poems full of mystery-
Intended to be read from Tréguier
To Paramaribo . . .
  "Ce qu'on dit au poète à propos
  des fleurs"

Rimbaud: Collected Poems
(Harmondsworth: Penguin, 1962)
Mona's original first name was contained in *Paramaribo*. I unconsciously associated it with Venice, which has the same assonance as her second first name and

Virile farewells in train stations, while these tall, thin travellers stand at the doors of the express trains that carry them away at a breathtaking speed towards their inaccessible women lovers; the wind blows their hair and freezes their temples, but they keep the same enigmatic and powerful smile for hours. And here they are already in the fan of the railroads, a lyrical symptom of the proximity of capitals.

The first illuminated signs, a streetcar that has broken down just at the turn of the outside boulevard, the public gardens the color of alcohol immediately gave them the distress of angels and the violence of the blind. The wind has died down: what does it matter — they now have the look of fabulous peddlers, their shirts open and with knitted eyebrows. The river is black and shiny enough this evening to reflect their nascent savagery. So they prefer neither the ocean at Tréguier, nor the secular hemorrhage of the Red Sea the length of the Arabian desert, but the almost immobile water of this river which they compare to a razor in several respects, and in no way lightly. [6]

It is daytime, but that solves nothing; for they then notice that they are unable to distinguish the florists' windows from the butchers' displays, and they take a very illegitimate pride in it, for there are some flowers they like.

Yes, each turn of the wheel had brought them closer to their inaccessible women lovers. They know this conse-

---

also refers to one of the main towns — Tréguier — of a country from where she had once written to me, this town also having the same initial syllable consonants as her surname (her husband's name), and being certainly unpleasant for me for this reason. When I noticed my mistake I was very careful to correct myself, and the word *Tréguier* could thus take on an importance that explains its present intervention.

crated formula and greatly appreciate its precision. In the morning fortunetellers had announced revenge, but this revenge, predicted at dawn, could certainly not affect the indifference of these adventurers: for since each turn of the wheel brought them closer to their inaccessible women lovers, their indifference was scientific.

"Triangles!" they cried, "scalene triangles! With your examples of equality, similarity, and dissimilarity, you form a metaphysics of ice, undoubtedly the coldest of all; but it is a wonderful piece of writing for our eyelids. The ice floe itself is less impersonal, and yet so many women have been solidified in it for centuries. In places where it is transparent, one can still catch sight of their imperishable flesh from time to time. But light-years have gone by over the ice floe; nothing, on the contrary, will ever be able to go by over you, triangles, first faces after ours, not even the fast express trains that carry us away. You alone give us a taste for indifference, and for realizing it, sleepwalking triangles, sheathed in red silk, wavering, lunatic triangles, heavy triangles. The light-years most certainly possess the charm of tidal waves, and we do not look down on them; but they can do nothing to you, triangles, whereas you can do everything to them. So when, among the listeners at the crossroads, we are waiting for a natural and troubling answer from the popular refrain to our most despairingly imperious questions, it is in you, tender triangles who know little delay, that we find, if not the reasons, then at least the strength not to disobey. And we have been in our lovers' towns for three days."

Thus spoke the merchants. The water was unable to open the eye and the light-years, like metal tears, flowed over the river, but without mixing in with it. The sea would no doubt absorb them; so no one was worried about their fate.

No one, not even those emphatic exiles who, even though they had organized the terror, did not know what to do with themselves. Space pursues them, surrounds them, digests them in a giant phagocytosis. Space has already replaced them. [7]

Friday, at the Sèvres-Babylone intersection, I negligently crumpled the flier that was negligently handed to me. But a few steps further on, feeling a sudden remorse, I wanted to read this square of crumpled paper attentively and humbly. In the upper left-hand corner, there was a stylized four-leafed clover bearing the inscription "I bring good luck."

This day was one of the unhappiest of my life and drove me to the only nervous breakdown I have ever had occasion to have. A punishment for my instinctive scorn of this ridiculous piece of paper, or a punishment for my ultimate submission; I am to this day still not permitted to choose. And yet the true value of these signs is not in the behavior that they determine, but in the fact that on the basis of the complex that they form together with this behavior, it is possible for everyone to take hold of the true ends and sources of his or her lyrical necessity, and by doing so to make life understand that, within the realm of poetry and of love, begging is not allowed.

★

---

[7] A transparent description of a psych-asthenic realization.

I walk to the end of a sea that is more unforeseeable
than myself. Just like yesterday, just like tomorrow, a
masked woman offers me with an outstretched arm the poi-
soned philter in which are dissolved the only advantages I
am anxious to reserve for myself.[8] *She is unable to dis-*
tinguish anything from a glove. Children with lips rotted
by ulcers and pustules kiss her incorruptible bosom.
Ultimately I do not need to live, which explains my con-
duct, my hatred for life's ruses . . .

So it is against such ruses that at the end of these pas-
sionate calculations I write the final identification: making love (faire l'amour) *and* playing dead (faire la mort).[9]

---

[8] The femme fatale theme; see chapter 3.

[9] It was thus that I was predisposed to being interested in praying mantises. See chapters 4 and 5.

AFTERWORD

FEAR AND TREMBLING IN THE AGE

OF SURREALISM

Denis Hollier

*She exhausts, she kills, and it only makes her
all the more beautiful.*

—Alfred de Musset

The work of Roger Caillois is hard to classify. It is not so much that, like the work of Bataille, Blanchot, or Sartre, it confuses and multiplies registers, genres, and styles, but more because of Caillois's perverse insistence on confining himself to the register of theory, at the expense of literature, even though he was also the author of works of fiction, such as the cunning rewriting of history that he staged in *Pontius Pilate*. His work suggests essentially negative reasons for such a choice. In all his essays, whether they deal with sociology or with aesthetics, with ethics or with natural history, there emerges in one way or another the same panicked fascination when confronted by the absolute power of the imagination, an imagination conceived of as a force of ontological leveling in which Caillois sees something like the Freudian death drive, but a death drive whose power of dissolution is still more radical than it was for Freud. This is because its domain is not limited to the psyche; as one draws near to it, the distinction between the psychological and the physical, between the exterior and the interior disappears, and the difference between I and not-I, between subject and object, is rendered obsolete. It is essential, according to Caillois, not to let oneself be swept away by this tidal wave in which all differences collapse: his choice of a theoretical style rather than a fictional one is grounded in his resistance to everything that gives in to the imagination. Just as a vigilant Ulysses, tied to the mast, could listen to the sirens without yielding to their song, the refusal of fiction allowed Caillois to draw closer to the imagination without losing himself within it.

But this theoretical style remains no less difficult to situate. Its defensive origins are undoubtedly responsible for what is heterodox, oblique, disquieting, and—one might even be justified in saying—hypocritical, in Caillois's relation to knowledge. In his texts, scientific discourse is rerouted toward much more unsettling and uncanny goals than that of the search for truth. It was Caillois, exiled in Buenos Aires during World War II, who made Borges known outside Argentina. Behind the mask of science, employed to repel the temptations of fiction but transforming knowledge into fiction's uncanny double, there is something that evokes Borges's imaginary encyclopedias. In a bizarre manner, this resistance to fiction exposes science to the shadowless light of the unreal, inoculating theory with the very fiction that theory was believed to immunize against.

The impression of uncanniness given by Caillois's work can also be felt in the simple difficulty of classifying him institutionally (he was neither an academic nor a journalist, neither a scientist nor a researcher, nor could he even be termed an "intellectual"). It is equally difficult to decide where this impression comes from, to say whether it corresponds to a judgment brought to the work from within or from without, whether it is the reader who imparts this judgment or if it is not rather the work itself that prompts it, whether this judgment is added to the work or is part of it. Indeed, this work could be described as a long meditation on the vertiginous experience of out-of-placeness, with the subject prey to the displacement of a writing over which he has no control, his place taken over by a space: the experience, that is, of a writing without a subject, of a grammatology prior to man. From one end of his work to the other, from *The Necessity of the Mind* to *The Writing of Stones*, Caillois pursues the misfit cogito of what the psychiatry of the time called psychasthenic, those "emphatic exiles," as he calls them, "who no longer know what to do with themselves."[1]

★　　★　　★

The Necessity of the Mind was published after his death in 1978. Caillois never made reference to this autobiographical essay, his first book, written when he was twenty years old. This discovery, however, was not the only surprise served up from beyond the grave by the publication of these youthful memoirs. *The Necessity of the Mind* does not merely exhume the unexpectedly young and autobiographical Caillois. It projects onto his first texts (in particular his famous essays on the praying mantis and the psychasthenic experience) an unusually autobiographical light, rooting their manifestoes of impersonality in the most personal of soils.

The surrealists, who idolized woman, wanted her to be "fatal." They expected of her that she would make them feel the fear and trembling that, in amplifying man's emotions, would raise them to the level of the sacred. In *Manhood*, Michel Leiris thus recalls the rage that overtook him one day when his father refused to share his admiration for two lines from *Alcools*, in which Apollinaire, conforming to this theory of the beautiful, makes the fear of woman the fundamental aesthetic affect: "This woman was so beautiful,/ That I was afraid of her." Caillois does not cite them, but we recognize a variation—conscious or not—on these same lines of "1909," in "women so beautiful as to inspire fear," which he mentions in one of his own poetic

---

[1] *The Writing of Stones*, trans. Barbara Bray (Charlottesville: University of Virginia Press, 1980). *The Necessity of the Mind* p. 149.

texts quoted in *The Necessity of the Mind*.[2] Beyond this shared reference, moreover, the autobiographies of Leiris and Caillois both invoke
muses who are, from this point of view, equally chilling. Leiris writes
Manhood under the spell of the figure of Judith who, after having let
herself be possessed by Holophernis, decapitates him. In *The Necessity
of the Mind* it is the female praying mantis—the Judith of the animal
kingdom from whom no male who penetrates her departs alive—who
drags Caillois into the quicksand of autobiography. His obsession with
both cannibal objects and invisible architecture allowed him to appreciate the fantasies awakened in Dali by what a felicitous catachresis
designates in French as the "mouths of the metro." There was a fascination around this time with oral masochism (Bachelard, in a study
on Leiris, describes a Jonah complex), and when Leiris and Caillois,
along with Bataille, were soon to organize the College of Sociology,
these fantasies would converge in the figure of Acéphale, the decapitated Don Juan.

Caillois published "The Praying Mantis" in two versions. The
first, which was illustrated, appeared in 1934 in the surrealist journal,
Minotaure. Its better-known version is the one he reworked four years
later for *Myth and Man*. *The Necessity of the Mind* allows a rediscovery
of the first version: its fifth chapter reprints it as is, even including the
footnote that, in *Minotaure*, had signaled that those pages make up
chapter 5 of a forthcoming work entitled *The Necessity of the Mind*. In
the *Minotaure* version, Caillois had announced: "I will speak of my
personal adventures later"; but it was not until the posthumous publication of *The Necessity of the Mind* that one was able to read them.

---

[2] *The Necessity of the Mind*, p. 61.
Caillois quotes, in the same vein, a line
by Alfred de Musset, in which, speaking
of a woman, the romantic poet sighs:
"She exhausts, she kills, and it only
makes her all the more beautiful" (*The
Necessity of the Mind*, p. 82 and p. 153).

Coming from the northeast of France (Reims), Caillois for some time had nothing but a bookish relation to the insect. It was in 1928 (when he was fifteen years old) that he saw his first mantis, while on vacation on a beach in the South of France. The same day a woman made advances to him, thus making two firsts in one day.

These brief indications lead one to meditate, first of all, on the rather surprising conjunction of the mantis and the autobiographical discourse, and second, on the effects this conjunction has on the text in which it occurs. One feels, indeed, a resolute defeatism in the fact that a man should choose to exhibit his first-person, to exhibit himself in the first person, in front of the mantis, this legendary man-eater. Moreover, the text, between its writing and its publication, is in fact subjected to a fate that illustrates the defeat of the first person quite literally: both versions of the essay published by Caillois during his lifetime suppress all personal references from the exposition of their themes. It is as if the autobiography had been sapped, dissolved from within, then assimilated by the third-person voice of the scientific study on the praying mantis. It is difficult not to be struck by the homology of a double disappearance that submits the first person of the author to the same fate as the male hero of the tragic love story he is telling. A strange *mise en abîme* folds the statement back into the utterance, stitches the fate of its subject (which does not reappear alive after having penetrated its female) onto the text itself (for once it has been written, it does not appear in published form), and programs the acting out of the disappearance it recounts. The praying mantis is the only survivor, both—as female—of the coitus and—as a scientific essay written in the third person—of the autobiography. The text's ingestion of its pretext thus creates only a repetition of the (nontextual) devouring of its sexual partner by the female. It is as if, for Caillois, the meeting with the mantis had resulted in the depersonalization of his voice; his first person, at least his literary first person, did not really survive *The Necessity of the Mind*.

In *Myth and Man* Caillois borrows Nietzsche's definition of myth

as that utterance that performs an *"orgiastische Selbstvernichtung."*[3]
With the mantis, this "orgiastic self-annihilation" occurs at two levels:
the self-annihilation of the male, who disappears in the act of copulation, and also the depersonalization of mythical utterance. From the
mantis as myth to the myth as discourse, the continuity is striking. The
mode of the discourse is homogenous with its contents. The praying
mantis thus superimposes the myth of defacement onto the myth as
defacement. Myth finds its allegorical fulfillment in the orgy by the
same means the male mantis achieves his self-effacement, his own self-
bracketing.

★　　　★　　　★

The fact that a text is posthumous is sufficient to give it an aura,
an autobiographical halo. In casting the text's final form, the death of
the author produces a shift from signs to event, tying together in a rare
convergence the web of language with that of life. However, the
posthumous status of *The Necessity of the Mind* is not the result of a
biographical accident. For it is a finished text. Posthumous and inaug-
ural, it is the first book that Caillois wrote. It happened that, scarcely
had it been written, than its author buried it. But scarcely had its author
been buried, than it appeared. Here the homology between the fate of
the text and that of the praying mantis stops, a homology that takes into
account only the first half of the history of the text. It is, in fact,
interesting that Caillois did not publish his autobiography. It is no less
interesting that he did not destroy it. Because if *The Necessity of the*

---

[3] *Le mythe et l'homme* (Paris: Gallimard,
1938), p. 25.

Mind had disappeared for real, the chances are very great that we would know nothing abut it. *The Necessity of the Mind* did not appear, but did not totally disappear either. In terms of a strategy that no longer suggests the fate of the male mantis, but rather the mimetic guile of the insects Caillois studies in the essay on psychasthenia, the first person is put on hold. Just as Ulysses did at his mast, the autobiography, faced with the praying mantis, played dead in order to survive as long as its author was alive.

The Necessity of the Mind is not, properly speaking, an autobiography. In the strong and quasi-chemical sense of the word *analysis,* it is rather more an experiment in autoanalysis. It is an exercise in the analysis of the self; an experience of the dissolution, the decomposition, performed in the first person on the first person; not only the tale of a crisis, but the putting of the ego into crisis. As such, it evokes the contemporary writings of young authors of the time who, like Sartre in *The Transcendence of the Ego,* in passages from *Nausea* and from "The Wall," try to depsychologize consciousness, to describe a consciousness cleansed of all subjectivity, what Blanchot would later call a consciousness without self (and even, more strangely, a self without self), a consciousness that would be that of no one. But *The Transcendence of the Ego* is a phenomenological essay, not an autobiography; the most vivid paradox of *The Necessity of the Mind* lies precisely in the fact that Caillois resorts to self-analysis to account for this dissolution of the self, that he gives the first person the task of formulating and even of producing the transcendence of the ego.

In this crisis of depersonalization, what is at stake is not (as with the praying mantis) the simple disappearance of the ego, but (as in mimicry) the ego's fascination for a world from which it will be absent, for a world in which there would be no place for it, in which it would be out of place. *The Necessity of the Mind* is the autobiography of a subject literally possessed by its own absence. A strangely posthumous first person allows the subject to shelter himself within his own absence, absent but in such a way as to be present at his own absence, simultaneously absent and the witness of this absence, witnessing *in absentia* (but nonetheless in the first person) his own absence, as if he had succeeded in disappearing without losing sight of himself, as if his absence, instead of denying, had confirmed the first person. This kind of ontological gymnastics leads to formulas such as "I wanted to cross the border of my skin, live on the other side of my sense."[4] Caillois admired the Montesquieu of the *Persian Letters* for having invented the art of "pretending to be foreign to the society one lives in": *The Necessity of the Mind* suggests an autobiographical revolution that, mirroring Montesquieu's sociological revolution, would allow a subject to feel, and even to become, foreign to the body it lives in, foreign to its own life.

The Necessity of the Mind owes much to *Nadja*. One day we will doubtless understand that autobiography was the great literary genre of surrealism. In saying this I am not thinking of retired surrealists who finished by reaching the age of writing their memoirs. On the contrary, the surrealist autobiographical essays are all youthful works, works of an insolent immaturity, surrealist above all—one might say—through their prematurity, their authors having rarely reached the age required for the practice of this type of exercise, the age when one has a life to recount. This is the case of André Breton, not only with *Nadja,* but also with *Les vases communicants* and *L'amour fou.* It is likewise true of Michel Leiris's *Manhood,* begun before he was thirty. As for Caillois, he almost needed a letter from his parents: not yet twenty years old,

---

[4] *The Necessity of the Mind,* p. 104.

traumatized by his first encounters with the female body, he began to write *The Necessity of the Mind.*

Autobiography here does not transmit the legacy of the experience of a life; it is the exercise of inexperience. The first person rushes to the front lines, effacing itself in manifesting itself, spending itself, the first victim of the epistemological break.

CONTENTS

Illustrations

Covers: Two photographs taken during surgery of the spinal
                        cord. Photo, Max Aguilera-Hellweg. All rights
                        reserved by the photographer.

Jacket: Congo Mantid in defensive posture. Photo,
                        Edward S. Ross.

Front endpaper: *Untitled* (1930). Photo, Jacques-André Boiffard.
                        Published in *Documents*.

Interior
illustrations:
                        Moth and candle. Photo, Brassai. Published in
                        Minotaure.

                        Jeunes grecs faisant battre des coqs (1846). Jean-
                        Léon Gérôme. Musée d'Orsay.

                        Acherontia (Death's Head Moth), Bandar Baru,
                        Sumatra. Photo, Edward S. Ross.

                        Torse II. Self-Portrait. Pierre Molinier.
                        Copyright 1990 ARS N.Y./SPADEM.

                        Self-Portraits; two with excised faces. Pierre
                        Molinier. Copyright 1990 ARS N.Y./SPADEM.

                        Au Revoir! Postcard marked "Printed in Prussia."
                        Date unknown.

                        Mantid portrait, *Litaneutria Obscura.* Photo,
                        Edward S. Ross.

Rear flyleaf: *Untitled* (1929). Jacques-André Boiffard.

Rear endpaper: Mantid. Photo, Dr. Eckehard Liske.

The Lapis Press
589 No. Venice Blvd.
Venice, CA 90291

Publisher
    Sam Francis

Translator
    Michael Syrotinski

Managing Editor
Visual Concept
    Robert Shapazian

Designer
    Patrick Dooley

The Publisher thanks Denis Hollier for his assistance in making this
book possible, and Edward S. Ross, California Academy of Sciences,
for his help in securing photographs.

This translation was assisted by a grant from the French Ministry
of Culture.

Published 1990

Printed in the United States of America.

La Nécessité d'esprit by Roger Caillois.
© Editions Gallimard, 1981

English translation copyright © 1990 by The Lapis Press

Afterword copyright © by Denis Hollier

ISBN 0-932499-40-6

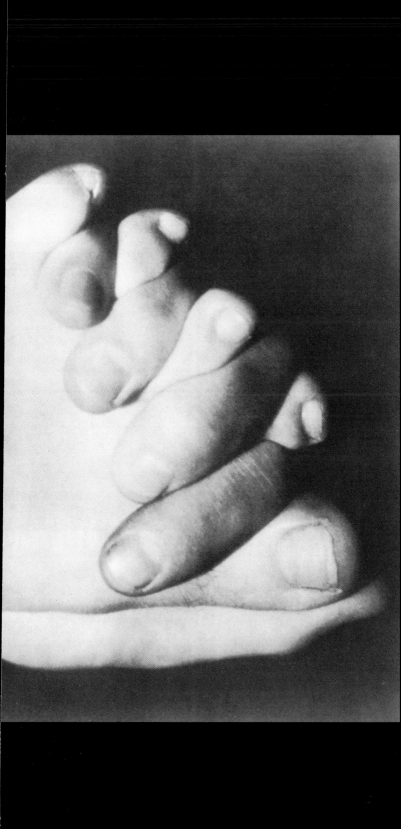